Our Stations and Places

Masonic Officers Handbook
by Henry G. Meacham
Revised and Expanded
by Michael R. Poll

Our Stations and Places
Masonic Officers Handbook
by Henry G. Meacham
Revised and expanded by Michael R. Poll

A Cornerstone Book
Published by Cornerstone Book Publishers
Copyright © 2007, 2014, 2019, & 2023 Cornerstone Book Publishers

Cornerstone Book Publishers
Hot Springs Village, AR

First Cornerstone Edition - 2007
Second Cornerstone Edition - 2014
Third Cornerstone Edition – 2019
Forth Cornerstone Revised Edition - 2023

www.cornerstonepublishers.com

ISBN: 978-1-934935-96-5

Dedication

*To the Seekers of Light and the souls
with a hunger to grow.*

Table of Contents

Foreword

In 1938, Henry G. Meacham published the first edition of *Our Stations and Places*. This present work is that first edition revised and expanded for best use in today's Freemasonry. The goal remains the same as in 1938; to provide assistance to Masonic lodges, through their officers, by the means of a clear and useful officer's handbook.

The original edition was written specifically for lodges under the jurisdiction of the Grand Lodge of New York. This edition was revised so that it can be put into use by lodges under any jurisdiction. The present edition was also expanded with the addition of a chapter on the various lodge committees and a collection of papers directly relevant to the subject of lodge improvement and understanding.

Our Stations and Places is a Masonic officer's tool. Like any tool, it is only beneficial if it is used. If you have the desire to be of service to your lodge and the willingness to apply your creative mind to the improvement of your lodge, then wonderful things can happen. The sky and your imagination are the limits.

This book is part of the Cornerstone Officer's Education Series alongside the Worshipful Master's parliamentary tool, *Robert's Rule of Order: Masonic Edition*.

We sincerely hope that you study and put this handbook to use in your lodge. Your singular effort to improve your lodge is vitally important to the whole of Freemasonry. Each single effort builds a solid foundation for the success of all our lodges.

Fraternally,
Michael R. Poll
Spring, 2007

Our Stations and Places

CHAPTER I
THE WORSHIPFUL MASTER

We often hear about the duty and prerogatives of the Worshipful Master and of things that he can do "to activate the particular group of brethren who compose his lodge." We also hear sighs, "If I were only young just for tonight," and thereby express, rather aptly, the state of mind of those who feel they have not taken advantage of all the opportunities presented during their lifetime. Things would be different (successful) if they could only be given a second chance.

We are living in the present, however, not in the past. What we do should be for today and the future. It is important that we turn our minds to some of those problems that a Warden must consider if he is to be a "good Master," problems that the Master must understand if he would possess those qualities of knowledge and leadership so essential for a successful Mastership.

Turn to the pages of your Grand Lodge Monitor generally titled "Prerogatives and Duties of the Worshipful Master." You will read something close to this in the introduction:

> "By the prerogatives of the Worshipful Master the inherent right and authority he possesses because of his position, giving him as it does, extraordinary powers and privileges, which belong to the presiding officer of few other associations. In all instances, his decision on points of order is final in the lodge, for it is a settled principle of Masonic law that no appeal can be taken to the lodge from the decision of the

Master. The Grand Lodge, or the Grand Master alone, can overrule his decision on any point of order."

The prerogatives of the Worshipful Master are so numerous and varied that only some of the principal ones are here presented."

We must wonder how many Masters and Wardens have read the above and how many have studied it. The statements represent an important stone in the foundation of Masonic knowledge, and with a careful perusal of his duties and prerogatives, as given in this part of your Monitor, is most essential to anyone anxious to be a success in the East.

Opening the lodge

Let me quote the third duty as herein given:

"To open his lodge at the time specified in the bylaws and do it at a suitable hour."

It would seem safe in asserting that no small amount of the failure of brethren to attend lodge may be ascribed to the lateness of the hour at which the Master calls his lodge to order — although the bylaws of the lodge say when lodge shall be opened. To cause brethren to stand around for half or three-quarters of an hour, waiting for the lodge to be opened when there seems to be no apparent reason for tardiness, does not encourage members to attend. It shows a considerable lack of concern for both the lodge and the brethren. Most people have a fair sense of time and punctuality, and many can be irked by being forced to wait for the Master, who, through lack of concern, fails to observe the much-needed factor of punctuality.

The conduct of the Worshipful Master often sets the tone for the conduct of the lodge. A Master who governs his actions responsibly and with the lodge's best interests in mind can inspire similar attitudes in the membership.

We may consider the Master a vitally important part of the educational department of the Grand Lodge.

The Work

> "To render the ritualistic work of the lodge and the brethren therein."

The Master should be, in fact, Master of the Work, competent to render every part thereof and, therefore, may be compared to the principal of a school. While he may not, himself, teach every candidate that comes into his lodge, he must make certain that the education given to each new Brother is a quality education.

The Master alone is responsible to the Grand Lodge for his lodge and must be competent to instruct his brethren. A Master who is not competent in the Work teaches that no one needs to be competent. The example set by the Master sets the tone for the lodge.

But what does it mean to be competent in the Work? Is "the Work" the words of the ritual alone, and is the limit of the Master's responsibility to know the words much as an actor is required to know his lines in a play?

Our Art can be understood as taking an imperfect human and attempting to teach him methods of improving his life. To represent this goal, we use the symbolism of working the Rough Ashlar into a more Perfect Ashlar. If the Master does not understand the meanings behind the words of the Work, then all he can teach is empty words. We might as well have a video of the ritual with a computer-generated Master in the East. The Work will be letter-perfect, but the video cannot answer questions or give any additional explanations to aid in understanding the Work. The Work will not be done.

One who accepts the office of Master should be well versed in both the proper words of the Work and the meaning of the words and various symbols. Only then can he be considered competent in the Work.

Notification and Summons

One of the standard prerogatives gives an interesting distinction between a "Notification" and a "Summons."

> "The distinction between a 'Notification' and a 'Summons' is so great that it is strange how many overlook it. The former issues from the Worshipful Master or the lodge and is practically an Invitation. It is at the option of the brethren receiving it to attend the meeting or not, as he pleases. But a 'Summons' comes directly under the province of his Order of Business, and for its neglect, he may be disciplined. To disobey a summons is a serious Masonic offense."

Take your mind to the Work of the Second and Third Degree, particularly that of the Second Degree, so that you may observe how this matter of the summons is emphasized. It is stressed purposely so that a strong impression may be made on the candidate's mind — and it should be equally emphatic to all the brethren.

The important distinction between a Notification and a Summons should be clearly understood, and a Warden who fixes it in his mind is taking an important step toward a proper understanding of his duties as Worshipful Master of his lodge. The Master who has fortified himself with a knowledge of this distinction and is duly impressed with its importance cannot fail to impress upon the minds of his brethren their responsibility in connection with a Summons.

The Minutes

It would be wise, too, that the Master of the lodge and the Secretary read the ninth duty.

> "To exercise Supervision over the minutes, that nothing improper be recorded, and nothing essential to a complete record be omitted."

It is the Worshipful Master who should supervise all aspects of the lodge operation, yet in some lodges, we see the Secretary "running the show." Each position's normal length of office might explain this shift of assumed authority. Most lodges allow a Worshipful Master to serve only one term (normally one year) at a time, but the Secretary is often elected to that position for a number of years. It is common to see a Secretary holding his office longer than the Worshipful Master has been a Mason. In reality, the Secretary is often the more experienced officer. In some cases, if the Secretary did not exercise his experience, the business of the lodge would suffer under an inexperienced Master incapable of properly fulfilling his duties.

A lodge does not benefit from a Worshipful Master ignorant of his duties or a Secretary operating under the belief that the Worshipful Master is his subordinate. In both cases, the answer is education.

CHAPTER II
COURTESIES OF THE EAST

"Courtesies of the East" — a phrase uttered by many Masters during the year. We might wonder if the phrase is not so often used as to lose its significance in the mind of the one employing it.

The question arises because the Spirit of the phrase is too frequently departed from, not so much in the matter of welcoming Worshipful, Right Worshipful, and Most Worshipful Brothers to the East, but in the entire business of making welcome brethren who come to render the lodge a definite service which they have been asked to perform.

Anyone who travels to more than a few lodges can discover cases of what amounts to down-right incivility — due without any doubt to simple thoughtlessness. One recent instance came to me of a brother who journeyed twenty-five miles to lecture at a lodge meeting. He was not invited to come early to be the guest of the Master, or the lodge, at dinner, and no offer was made to pay his expenses. The visiting brother arrived at the suggested hour of nine but was kept in the ante-room until ten o'clock. When he was called in, and after a quick expression of thanks, the brother was told that owing to the lateness of the hour and his probably wanting to get home at a reasonable hour, he might want to curtail his remarks. Incredible!

Happily, this instance does not represent a universally accepted condition among our lodges. Still, it is a far too prevalent condition and should not exist in any lodge. Anyone who has served several years in the various chairs of his lodge should have become sensitive to those amenities, which should make a visitor happy for the giving of his effort.

Another instance I am aware of is a busy clergyman who took time to travel a good distance one evening to deliver an address in a lodge, only to be met by an examining committee who "put him through the paces." Questions that had no possible bearing on the man's admissibility into a Masonic lodge were asked. When the visitor was permitted to ask some Masonic questions on his part, not only did the committee not answer his questions, but the committee introduced him to the lodge with statements that attempted to hold him up to ridicule. It was later pointed out that the committee did not know he was the visiting speaker. Instead of that being an extenuating fact, this only emphasizes that *every* visitor should expect and receive every possible courtesy from the East (as well as those acting on behalf of the East). Again, in this case, no suggestion was made by the lodge to compensate him for the expenses involved in getting to and from the lodge.

In another kind of case, a brother in very considerable demand as a speaker was asked to give one of his addresses to a lodge. The brother remained in town for the occasion, ate alone, received no dinner invitation, and showed up at the lodge at nine o'clock. He was received in the lodge and sat on the sidelines until after eleven o'clock, when, after a long business session, the Master announced: "And now, brethren, Brother .... has a message that he wants to deliver to us." That terse remark constituted his introduction to his audience. Likewise, this night a soloist had been asked to come and render two or three numbers. Although singing was his vocation, he was permitted to come to town, also buy his dinner, and then, along with the speaker, permitted to withdraw after the event. And afterward, with the speaker, he was not to receive so much as a word of appreciation for his efforts.

Other similar cases could be related, but these are sufficient to indicate how extraordinarily lacking some Worshipful Masters are in visitors' simplest amenities of life. It is not enough to assume that, since all are Masons and brothers together, the ordinary courtesies of human relationships need not be observed. It is an old joke that members of families can ride roughshod over the sensibilities of one another. In the best of families, it is not done, and if a lodge considers itself a family, the Master should at least conduct the affairs of the lodge on the assumption that it is a fine family.

A few simple principles may be laid down to govern such cases. First, the speaker, entertainer, or otherwise, should receive a letter expressing the Master's appreciation at least a week before the meeting date. The letter should cover all arrangements, including a dinner invitation, the time and place, and an offer of transportation to and from the meeting. Also included in the letter should be whether the dress is formal or business clothes, and the place in the evening's program that the visitor is to occupy should be covered. In addition, an offer should be made to cover the visitors' expenses. If the guest is from out of town, a hotel room should be provided. If the lodge does not have the funds to pay such an expense, then a collection should be made of the members at the time of the meeting to help the visitor with this expense. If the visitor is local, then some gift should be given to him from the lodge as a "thank you" for his effort.

If the speaker does not accept the invitation to dinner but is to show up at the lodge at a certain hour, full instructions should be left with the Tyler that the Master or the committee be notified immediately upon his arrival. If he is not brought directly into the lodge, he should not be allowed to cool his heels alone in the anti-room, but a committee member should be sent out to greet him and remain with him until his entrance into the lodge.

Nor should any visitor be permitted to enter the lodge alone. He should be given the consideration of an escort, with a fitting presentation, and taken to the East to be presented to the lodge in a courteous and kindly manner. Greetings by the Master should not be excessive but sufficiently cordial to make the visitor feel at home and welcome. It costs nothing to be friendly. Often how a visiting speaker is received spells the difference between a good address and an indifferent one, in other words, a speaker on coming to a lodge should be made to feel that he is the attraction, as he undoubtedly should be, of the evening.

One must regret that a statement of simple principle or courtesy should be necessary. In the olden days, the Operative Mason spent an apprenticeship of seven years to learn the principles of his Craft. Today, Speculative Masons spend a lifetime perfecting the human temple through character and personality development. Training in such points as the above is not to be achieved, I suppose, in a year or two years, but it is an ideal to be pursued. I know of no place in a Mason's career that affords so perfect a training school as the Mastership. The Master who fails to make the most of his office as a school, among other things of deportment, misses vastly more than he can afford to miss.

CHAPTER III
THE SECRETS OF THE CHAIR

The glowing radiance of the Masonic Temple in the little town shone brightly that January night. The single blue light over the entrance beckoned to the groups making their way to their Mecca — the lodge room. The Brothers wore their heavy clothing, for the weather was intensely cold. Occasionally a pair of snowshoes could be seen tucked under the arm of the bearer — not needed now on the cleared walks of the town, but necessary in the deep snow of the surrounding hills. Alone and in groups, they came, stamping the snow from their feet as they entered the building. Then ascending the stairs to the upper floor, where wraps were removed, snowshoes stacked in the corner, and fingers toasted at the glowing stove.

The buzz of conversation and the peals of laughter evoked from time to time by good-natured banter grew in heartiness as new groups filtered in. It was a scene familiar to each brother present. And yet something seemed different. Maybe it was the brethren who attended the lodge but once or twice a year. Be that as it may, all of those present seemed expectant, as if something unusual was about to happen.

It was Installation Night!

A sudden hush as the gavel fell! Groups broke away to the chairs on the sides. Officers took their respective stations and places. The lodge was opened in due form with the Worshipful Master officiating for the last time. Routine matters were attended to, and under "New Business," the East announced that officers for the ensuing year would be installed. The Worshipful Master announced, too, that the

Master-elect, before his installation, would be invested with the Secrets of the Chair. In view of the Master and the Past Masters, but out of view of the other Members, the investiture of the Master-elect took place. Then the Worshipful Master installed his successor and the other officers of the lodge.

This picture of installation night shows that the retiring Master validates his successor by investing him with the Secrets of the Chair before installing him — and, of course, this may be accomplished by a group investiture as is done in so many jurisdictions. It is this simple investiture to which I wish to call attention. Many members of the Craft have a misconception concerning this ceremony. Some say that if the Master-elect of a lodge has had the Past Master Degree in a Chapter of Royal Arch Masons, he does not need to be invested. Nor does it stop there, for Past Master's Associations have been known to exemplify what they call the "Past Master Degree," believing this is identical to the investiture. This condition exists not because of a willful disregard for a time-honored practice and requirement but because of a possible lack of authentic information.

Worshipful Masters too frequently neglect this branch of Masonic education. His investiture should always precede the installation of the Worshipful Master.

For as long as Freemasonry has been an organized fraternity, it has been deemed needful to put each Master, before his installation, in possession of what is known as the "Secrets of the Chair." These "Secrets" consist of information and minor ritual, where none but actual Past Masters, or Masters vouched for as such, are permitted to witness or hear.

Symbolic Masonry has only three Degrees — Entered Apprentice, Fellowcraft, and Master Mason. Where it has been taken over by Capitular Masonry and conferred under its jurisdiction only, the "Past Master" Degree legitimizes all candidates for the Royal Arch Degree. It was required that none could receive the Degree of Royal Arch except Past Masters. In Masonic writings, the Past Master of a Symbolic Lodge is known as an "actual" Past Master, and he who receives the degree of Past Master in a Chapter of the Royal Arch body as a "virtual" Past Master. To use the ceremony of a degree of a body outside the craft lodge is to subordinate Symbolic Masonry to that body — an act utterly wrong in principle and useless regarding any possible Constitutional requirement.

It is always difficult to put one's finger precisely on the spot where fallacies common to human organizations are born. Possibly Mackey, in his classic "Encyclopedia of Freemasonry," is partly to blame for the widespread confusion of this point. In that useful work, under the caption "Past Master," Mackey says:

"Past Master — An Honorary Degree conferred on the Master of a lodge at his installation into office. In this degree, the necessary instructions are conferred respecting the various ceremonies of the Order, such as installations, processions, the laying of cornerstones, etc. When a brother who has never before presided has been elected Master of a lodge, an emergent Lodge of Past Masters, consisting of not less than three, is convened, and all but Past Masters retiring, the degree is conferred upon the newly elected officer."

In this, Mackey is entirely wrong. Above all things, the Chapter work is not, and must not be, used at the Instillation of a Master-elect. No Chapter Mason who has not been installed as Master of a symbolic lodge would be permitted to be present when the Secrets of the chair are imparted to the Master-elect. After that quiet ceremony, the installation in the lodge room proceeds and any Master Mason in good standing may be present. What should be emphasized to the Craft is this: Symbolic Masonry is one thing, and Capitular Masonry is another. Above all else, Symbolic (or Craft, or Blue Lodge) Masonry is the foundation upon which all bodies and rites must rest. He, a Master Mason, possesses the ranking degree of the Craft. If he receives any additional degrees or honors by virtue of his membership in the lodge, that is, of course, his privilege, and only because he is a Master Mason. He can no more bring his Chapter to work into the lodge or take himself any privilege because he is a member of that body than he could bring in any of the features or titles belonging to the many other bodies depending on their membership on the mother body, namely, Craft Masonry.

Such are the facts. Let us not be misled. Let us take the time to search out the truth and, for all time, dismiss from our minds the travesty of the "Past Master Degree."

Not long ago, a Past Grand Master said that one of the great dangers of the Craft lay in the self-complacency of its members. He was right. We are too content to sit idly by and let the other Brother bear all the burden. All cannot be leaders, but all can work, and above all, each of us can have a firm reason for our Masonic membership. Let us not be complacent about this important Masonic ceremony and educational lesson. All of us, particularly if we are Past Masters, should make it a point to be sure that all new Masters are being properly invested with the Secrets of the Chair.

CHAPTER IV
THE MASTERSHIP AND THE BOARD

This is an age of keen competition in every human undertaking. We find the terrific struggle for existence in business, in things spiritual, and intellectual — in all pursuits of whatever nature.

This is frequently said to be the age during which fraternalism will end. I often smile when I hear this statement, for I believe it to be no truer now than at any other time. There are many more distractions today than ever before, but there are also ways of awakening interest in those things of the spirit for which at least our own fraternity stands. In other words, we have developed a defense against those influences that distract us. One important line of this defense is a Board of General Activities.

Many years ago, the Grand Lodge of New York formed a Bureau of Social and Educational Service. This was done to stimulate those near dormant lodges by setting up programs that would inspire their members to attend more frequently. This was accomplished through speakers who furnished the Masters with programs for special occasions. The goal was to help them foster Freemasonry in their brethren's hearts by grounding them in the ancient teachings of the Craft. It also provided a sound source to the brethren regarding Masonry's symbolism, landmarks, Masonic law, allegory, history, etc. The Bureau was the forerunner of the Grand Lodge of New York's present Board of General Activities. Their work is important, and many other jurisdictions have like services.

We have, of course, a wide variety of Masters. Some are sufficiently interested in their Masonic Work to do what is necessary to energize their lodges. Unfortunately, we also have lodges that have Masters who are indifferent, who are not leaders, or who do not care. With Masters of this latter kind, little can be done. We have such Masters with us always — they come and go, and "the place thereof knows them no more." They contribute nothing because they lack the basic qualities of leadership. But, given a Master who shows signs of life and such a Board allowed going to work, the result is always worthwhile.

My Brethren, if there is one thing this Craft needs more than anything else, it is to be roused from dormancy — where we too often find it. We need Masters who avidly grasp the opportunity given to them to serve. We need leadership by men with imagination. The man without a sense of humor and lively imagination is to be pitied. Imagination is a great factor in the progress of an individual and that of an organization. great leaders are, without exception, men of imagination.

Let us look for a moment at the Master who has these qualifications but is so very enthusiastic that this runs away with his good sense. Here a little sound judgment is needed to serve as a balance wheel. Such a Master is liable to transgress certain fundamentals because he is not well grounded in Masonry or because of excessive enthusiasm. His energies are apt to dissipate into thin air because they lack substance.

Now, is there a happy medium? Can these two divergent types of men reach a middle ground that will be safe and useful? My answer to these two questions is that interested Masons should look at the various boards or committees a Grand Lodge may have to deal with education.

The wise Master will go to this type of service committee because, my brother, their plans work and are essentially practical. I know they work because I have tried them and have seen them tried.

Let me tell a true story. A certain Senior Warden of an average lodge noticed some literature dealing with the service of the Board. He became interested because here he found the answer to a problem he had observed in nearly every lodge he knew anything about or had visited. He said nothing to any of the brethren of his lodge as they were inclined to look at him with disapproval as one possessing too much zeal. However, he sent for some of the literature, studied it, and, when finally elected Master, put some of the plans calculated to create new interest in his lodge into practice. He knew that because of business conditions in his community, there would be few candidates. He raised one man. But he doubled the average attendance at the regular communications!

When he was Senior Warden, this man had determined that if his lodge did not grow numerically during his year, he would at least cause it to grow spiritually. He determined that his one year in the East would be a year of growth for him and for his lodge. He realized that as one helps others to grow, he increases his own internal stature. So, while he was still Senior Warden, he started to look about him to see what could be done and how best he could do it. He studied his membership rolls. He found one of the brethren who played the cello. Two more were discovered who played the violin, and these three, with the pianist of the lodge, he encouraged to form a quartet. This performed so well that the brethren were able at every communication to listen to music that members of the lodge performed. And these men were given something to do. The members were given something for which to come to the lodge. They came again. They kept coming, and the word went out that anyone who missed a regular communication of this lodge was missing something worthwhile.

And so it went. The Board gave this Master the same encouragement with respect to speakers so that the Master could introduce to his brethren, on many a night, some speaker who had been selected with care so that nothing should be presented that was not in keeping with good Masonic tradition and practice. These speakers were Masons who were outstanding in their particular field. Each speaker gave something worthwhile to the lodge.

Also, while Senior Warden, this man discovered a copy of the Book of Constitutions of his Grand Lodge. He read it and then reread it to his brethren, a little at a time each night, until he had covered all those points in which he felt the lodge should be especially interested. The brethren liked it — to his utter amazement, they were interested far and above his fondest hopes.

And so it was during the entire year. Of course, some said, "It hasn't been done before. Therefore, it can't be done now." Soon, however, even these skeptics were silenced, with everybody getting back to the energetic Master and responding to him with words of encouragement.

What that man did, you can do — and much more. Today, we have at our fingertip's worthy material offered even on the internet that would cause our brethren of just a few years ago to gasp in amazement. Worshipful Master, why not see what is of value and try them? Why spend time and energy to contrive that which is already planned for you and probably planned far better than you could devise? You may alter these plans to fit the needs of your lodge or body, but at least you should try things that are practical and free for the asking.

And while we are on this subject, let us get straight to another point. The business of study clubs, the reading of

Masonic books, and more intensive efforts along all Masonic lines are not offered so that men should be led to forsake all other kinds of institutions. That is not the goal at all. Occasionally, I hear a man say that his lodge is his church and that he needs to be no better man than he will be if he follows the teachings of Masonry. This man has not stopped to reason the thing through. Such a conclusion is the result of shallow thinking. It was never intended that Freemasonry should take the place of the church, but a man should be a better churchman because he is a Mason.

So, what you make of your year as Master is up to you. If you use your imagination, temper it with reason, and build your year on a foundation of planning and study, you can do wonderful things. If your Grand lodge has a board or committee of general activities or the like, use them. If not, take a tour of the amazing study and planning program available on the internet. If you view your year in the East as one to provide service rather than a feather in your cap, you can serve in a manner that honors your office.

CHAPTER V
THE SENIOR WARDEN

The Gentle Art of Meditation, when applied to the ritual of Craft Masonry, never fails to reveal new beauties and new meanings that otherwise would escape us. Many a passage, otherwise obscure, is made instantly clear to be seen as clothed with the deepest significance. Hidden truths stand revealed. The relationship of this passage or to some other passage becomes apparent, and, as a result, enters into our Masonic experience a new and richer comprehension of the work. We are made to see how every detail of the work is embedded in the history, symbolism, and law of the Craft.

With this in mind, let us meditate for a little while upon the Senior Warden and his office, considering his part in the lodge work, especially as specified by the ritual and the law. And when I speak of the law, I mean our Masonic law.

The Senior Warden's first duty in the lodge is specified in the opening ceremony. Here he recites the reason for being in the West. But, like a clock ticking, of which we are seldom conscious, the deeper meaning is apt to escape us because we often hear it. Let us analyze his statement, then, to understand his duty better.

He is asked if he is satisfied with those present in the lodge. This means that here is the very place where caution begins. A definite responsibility is laid upon the shoulders of the Senior Warden. Having referred the matter to the proper officer, the Senior Warden reports, and he should know of which he speaks! He is responsible for guarding the lodge against the presence of cowans or eavesdroppers. This little ceremony, performed under his supervision, permits no laxity whatever in the carrying out of his duty.

In this regard alone, the Senior Warden owes to his lodge his supreme effort for the utmost faithfulness in performing his duty. The Worshipful Master, if he takes his work seriously, is a busy man, and it is natural enough that the important task of purging the lodge be delegated to the watchful care of the Senior Warden, who, informed upon the duty committed to his care, assures the Worshipful Master that all present are Master Masons.

The Senior Warden should never regard this duty as a perfunctory thing; never should it be simply assumed that all present are Master Masons. He must perform his duty with rigorous attention to every detail while preserving the respect due each member. At his installation, he hears the admonition, "Look well to the West," and here is an opportunity to display a praiseworthy zeal for the welfare of his lodge.

An old Past Master once told me of a Senior Warden whom he had known in days gone by. Never did the brother take anything for granted. Even so, his lodge was thoroughly purged that all present were in good standing. At times the brethren thought him too severe, but ultimately, they came to see the wisdom of his practice. No one ever sat in his lodge who was not entitled. And the lodge was better, this old Past Master told me, for the true Masonic zeal of his Senior Warden.

We now come to the second point having to do with the duty of the Senior Warden. First, he assists the Worshipful

Master; second, he seeks to promote harmony, which is the support of all institutions, "especially this of ours."

Here lies one of the Senior Warden's most important duties, if not the most important. As a lodge, we cannot accomplish anything without harmony. Too often have we seen the devastating effect of lack of harmony in a lodge. The very cornerstone upon which Masonry exists is goodwill among men. Banish harmony, and nothing is left but the dry, empty shell, the discarded husk from which nothing can grow. In our strong lodges, harmony may be found. In our useful lodges, those that are a powerful force in their communities, it is always found. Weak lodges are so because they either fail to develop their latent strength, or they do not work well together and have split into factions.

How utterly ridiculous a Masonic lodge must appear to the non-Mason who hears reports of turbulence or disagreements at our meetings. And, Bro. Senior Warden, I believe the very keynote of your station in the West is just at this point. Harmony can only be achieved and preserved if we live, think, and act as Brothers. We must practice forbearance, which includes the God-given traits of "patience" and "tact." I often wonder if the Almighty ever gave mankind more soothing influences than is summed up in those two words. The lodge that functions with the smoothness of a well-oiled machine, each part lending itself to the complete and harmonious movement of the whole, is a happy lodge.

And the Senior Warden is to assist the Worshipful Master. I think every Mason who considers the Senior Warden as such does so in the light of his qualifications for the East. If the Worshipful Master is absent from a communication, the Senior Warden presides over the lodge. What finer training school for the East could one pass than service in the West?

Here he may learn to assist without taking the lead. Here he may learn to act and develop those qualities of mind which, in a broad sense, will make him most useful. At any time, he may have to preside over the lodge, wherefore he should be as well informed of the ritual as the Master himself. And not the ritual alone! He should also be a student of the Grand Lodge Constitutions, rules, and laws. In this way, he may save the Worshipful Master and lodge much embarrassment. It is a duty that every Master, as well as the Senior and Junior Wardens, owe to the Craft. The great truth is that no human institution, Freemasonry included, is greater than the quality of its leadership. The higher the standard of our leadership in the East, the more valuable our lodges will be in service to our fellow man.

Another duty of the Senior Warden is to represent his lodge in the Grand Lodge should the Master not attend. It is almost inconceivable to imagine a Worshipful Master who fails to give his lodge representation in the Grand Body. If circumstances prevent his attendance, he should see that a Warden or a proxy attends.

When the Senior Warden represents his lodge at Grand Lodge, he should give a report to the lodge of the proceedings, just as the Master would have done. This report should be supplemented by reading to the brethren from the Transactions when received, from which a liberal education in Masonic practices may be obtained. Too seldom is a lodge bookcase containing bound volumes of the Grand Lodge Transactions or Proceedings, extending back for a number of years, where the brethren may have access to them. This valuable book too infrequently finds its way into the lodge room, where it belongs by every right.

Thus does the ritual, as we contemplate it, emphasize the work of the Senior Warden, giving it awe that perhaps we had not noticed before. For upon this officer rests a task of the utmost importance. And his conception of his duty to his brethren depends much on its usefulness as a character-forming and character-building institution.

CHAPTER VI
WHY IN THE WEST?

In considering those qualities of mind that ready a man to be Master of a Masonic lodge, one will think not only of the Worshipful Master but of the two Wardens as well. One thinks, indeed, of the Wardens in terms of the Master and asks, "What sort of Master will that Warden be"? What qualities does he have that qualify him for the responsibility ahead? What is he doing to qualify himself? How is he developing himself?

We have every right to expect a man to grow as he advances, and in this, the man himself plays a tremendous part. What is the measure of this future Master? Will he display an energetic interest in the performance of his work? Has he judgment and tact?

All these questions suggest themselves in the contemplation of these three officers. We cannot think of one without considering the other two, but let us focus on the middleman, the Senior Warden — though, of course, we shall have to speak of the Master and the Junior Warden, too. The three form a kind of triad functioning together in such a manner as to set to the whole lodge an example in harmony and coordination of effort. At any time, the Senior Warden may be called upon to preside in the absence of the Master, while the Junior Warden may find himself in the East if both of his superior officers are absent. The qualities of one, therefore, may be said aptly to be the qualities of the other. Here I wish to focus upon what a Senior Warden must do to equip himself for the East and upon what he has already done to qualify himself for the West.

It seems to me that the first fundamental is ritual. I say that because I know of no more fitting medium for a common understanding of Freemasonry. Ritual is the flawless language of Freemasonry, and he who would understand the Craft must first speak its language. Through the chairs, the Senior Warden has been speaking this language. By the time he reaches the station of Junior Warden, fresh from the experience of Senior Deacon, he ought to be familiar with the ritualistic work of every lodge office. It is to be taken for granted, too, that he knows the details of the floor work. He is well acquainted with the lodge membership; his vision is broader, and he is now looking at the Craft, not with one pair of eyes, but through the eyes of the entire lodge. No man can be skilled in the work of the Senior Warden and be narrow in his judgment of the members of his lodge.

But there is another fundamental of great importance. It is one that the Senior Warden must give his endless attention, and the Master must be a constant student. I allude to the Book of Constitutions. I mention this as the second of these great requisites. But too often I see examples of inexcusable ignorance on the part of those whose duty is to be informed. Some kinds of ignorance may be excused, others are inexcusable. Never has there been a time in the history of Freemasonry, I believe, when ignorance of the Craft was so inexcusable as now because more facilities are at hand than ever before to inform and instruct.

The constant study of your Book of Constitutions and Regulations is as necessary for the two Wardens as for the Worshipful Master. When called upon to preside, the Senior Warden must know how to handle an objection for a demand for the ballot, to name but one of many problems that may arise. The more diligently the Senior Warden applies himself to the study of the Constitutions and familiarizes himself with our common law, the easier will be his task when he becomes Master.

This preparation must not be left as a last-minute job. A man who worked in the same office once told me that he never prepared himself for a task ahead until it came his way. Maybe that is why he never advanced far!

I knew a Master who read to his lodge, a little at each communication, from the Book of Constitutions. He was amazed at the interest displayed. Brethren are keenly interested, universally so. And they have confidence and respect for the officer presiding in the East who knows what is proper from the legal standpoint. The foundation stone of knowledge is mighty comforting to one's feet, but one must place it there himself.

The third great fundamental requirement is an aptitude for furthering harmony in the lodge. A Grand Master once said that the lodge in which there is no harmony is un-Masonic. A Warden or a Master can better attain harmony if proficient in the first two requirements mentioned.

I touched on the need to be well acquainted with the membership. This is necessary to understand men's minds and how they work. We designate this fundamental as understanding the individuality of his lodge. Lodges differ, one from another, just as people differ. Here is an opportunity to study an interesting subject — just one of the many that come the way of the Senior Warden.

In his ritualistic work, in both the lodge's opening and closing, the Senior Warden mentions the great importance of harmony. He states that it is the support of all institutions and then brings in with special significance the part played by harmony in the affairs of the lodge.

He must study, then, its exemplification, not only in the lodge but also in the world. It is his duty to do everything to promote harmony in his life as an example of this virtue to others. Rarely do we meet a bit of English phrasing so utterly appropriate to the purpose for which it is designed as our ritual of Symbolic Masonry? The delicacy with which this matter of harmony is brought into the picture has charm and is as important as beautiful.

This theme of harmony is woven as a motif of our nature. And the Senior Warden is the first officer to mention it! This should teach our good friend in the West that he exemplifies this virtue.

Now that we have reviewed certain fundamentals in which the Senior Warden must be trained, we consider those broader affairs of which these things are merely the foundation. I alluded to the executive and the administrative phases of the Warden's chair, which are so important in fitting himself for the station of Worshipful Master. The Mastership is a station of clear tremendous responsibility to be approached with modesty, respect, and a clear desire to serve. The Master is responsible to the Grand Lodge for his acts as Master, but if the Senior or the Junior Warden presides at any time, the Master is still responsible for their acts. So, we may readily see how thoroughly schooled the Wardens should be to preside in a way that will not embarrass the Master.

Therefore, the Senior Warden, the second in command, is to be considered as a future presiding officer, not as one who merely stands in the West to rattle off a bit of ritual. He is the future Master and must possess those qualities of mind and spirit that will make him deeply sensible of the seriousness of the task that someday may be his.

All I have said above is designed merely to pave the way to a new point of view of the Senior Warden's duty. This is an office of deep importance. The development of the man, his outlook on life, how he takes hold, whether his enthusiasm is tempered with sound judgment — all these and much more will determine whether he will bring honor to the East and serve his lodge well.

Brother Senior Warden, look well to the West! This section has tried to set forth some things that will be useful for you to know. Much you must discover for yourself. And in enlarging your vision, you will find yourself a bigger man, spiritually and intellectually.

That is why you are in the West and have made a pilgrimage through the lodge chairs — that might have the opportunity of "growing into" the East as Worshipful Master.

Brother Senior Warden look well to the West!

CHAPTER VII
THE JUNIOR WARDEN

Occasionally one hears the opinion that sociability and entertainment as part of lodge activity is a new thing and a kind of innovation beneath Freemasonry's dignity. The truth is that "refreshment" is as old as the Craft itself, and a part of its original design. So, a lodge ignoring it falls below the ideal. This is proved by the fact that the custody of social activities is placed in the hands of one of the principal officers of the lodge, the Junior Warden, and it is further presupposed that he will have so much to do that he is given two Stewards to assist him.

The two Stewards, under the supervision of the Junior Warden, is the real "social committee" of a lodge. If these three officers were to do what is intended for them to do, there may be no need for any other committee. Furthermore, it is presupposed that refreshment will be understood to be the necessary relief so that work does not become drudgery. It is that balance between refreshment and work overseen by the Junior Warden. He is responsible for ensuring that we do not neglect our work by either the failure to refresh ourselves or by indulging in refreshment to the point of neglecting all else. He is truly in charge of equilibrium necessary for the high plane on which Freemasonry moves.

You may find in your jurisdiction's Monitor that,

"...three great Pillars support a lodge. These are denominated Wisdom, Strength, and Beauty — for there should be wisdom to contrive, strength to support, and beauty to adorn all great and important undertakings. They are represented by the three principal officers of the lodge — the Pillar of Wisdom by the Worshipful Master in the East, who is presumed to have the wisdom to open and govern the lodge; the Pillar of Strength by the Senior Warden in the West, whose duty it is to assist the Worshipful Master in the discharge of his arduous duties; the Pillar of Beauty by the Junior Warden in the South, whose duty it is to call the Craft from labor to refreshment, superintend them during the hours thereof, carefully to observe that the means of refreshment are not perverted to intemperance or excess, see that they return to their labor in due season, that the Worshipful Master may receive honor, and they pleasure and profit thereby."

These three Pillars symbolize the essentials of the nobility of character. Wisdom and Strength are incomplete without each other, Wisdom being necessary to direct Strength and Strength necessary in upholding that which is wise and good. And the Pillar of Beauty is a composite of the other two. Occasionally one meets a man with that clarity of vision which enables him, with apparent infallibility, to see the best course to pursue in any given situation. He can differentiate between those things that uplift and those that do not, and having the strength of character enables him to cling to the good. In this blending of Wisdom and Strength is to be found Beauty of character.

No wonder, then, that the Pillar of Beauty is placed in the South midway between the East and the West, exemplified by the Junior Warden. "To observe the sun at meridian, which is the glory and beauty of the day" — the very thought of Beauty itself is suggested in the recital of the officer's duty. The sun at the meridian, that point of greatest heat and light whence all living things receive strength to grow! That phrase can teach us that by seeking those qualities of mind represented by the Pillar of Beauty, we may hope to grow in Wisdom and Strength, becoming increasingly helpful to those about us.

The enduring quality of Beauty is emphasized by the fact that in many jurisdictions, the Master and Wardens of a lodge cannot resign. Thus, our brother in the South should consider wisely before accepting this Station and, having been installed, should show strength of purpose in properly performing his duties. In most lodges, the Junior Warden is one of the five lodge officers chosen annually by ballot, the other four being the Master, Senior Warden, Treasurer, and Secretary. In most jurisdictions, one must have served at least one year as a Warden before becoming Master. Experience has shown the importance of training in the West and South as preparation for the onerous duties of the East.

Again, the Junior Warden supervises the Craft while at refreshment. This does not mean he must remain at his Station during this period. Nor are we to suppose that brethren leaving or entering the lodge room during refreshment are to salute him. Neither the Altar nor the Three Great Lights are to be turned to face his Station at any time. In some jurisdictions, the Junior Warden, during refreshment, should mingle with those over whom he has supervision; otherwise, how can he be informed as to the means of refreshment?

Lodge's social activities come under his supervision. He has before him two Stewards whose duty it is "to provide for the Craft while at refreshment that the harmony and decorum thereof shall not be disturbed, and that when labor shall be resumed, the Worshipful Master may have honor and the Craft pleasure and profit therefrom." So reads the installation of the Stewards in various Monitors; here may the Stewards contemplate the significance of the Pillar of Beauty and how appropriate it is that they be placed with him in the South! Providing proper refreshment and supervision during the hours thereof is no idle task. In their functions, the Junior Warden and the Stewards are the lodge's social committee.

Consider, too, the duty of the Junior Warden in its legal aspect (the exact wording may vary from jurisdiction to jurisdiction):

> "In case of the absence or disability of the Master or a vacancy in his office, the Senior and Junior Wardens shall, in succession, succeed to his prerogatives and duties for all purposes, except for the installation of officers. In the absence of the Master and Wardens, a lodge cannot be opened except as herein provided."

In most jurisdictions, another legal aspect of the Junior Warden is the serious duty of being the officer to receive Masonic charges filed against any lodge member (Master excepted). The Junior Warden must be fully aware of and competent in the Grand Lodge's Book of Law, its Constitutions, and any other Rules that apply to Masonic jurisprudence. The Grand Lodge spells out the duties of the Junior Warden in this regard, and no Junior Warden should fail to refer to these laws in the event of charges being filed against a lodge Member. Masonry has no place for those of ill character. With only the best interest of Masonry itself, without regard to personal likes or dislikes, and with 100% compliance with Grand Lodge law, the Junior Warden should complete his duties in this sometimes extremely difficult duty.

In all aspects, we see that by adding to his "wisdom" and increasing his "strength" as a supporter of the lodge, the

Junior Warden will be as fully informed concerning the Ritual and the Grand Lodge *Constitutions* as the Master or Senior Warden. He may, at any time, without previous notice, be called upon to preside over the lodge and must never embarrass the lodge by ignorance concerning any duty that may confront him.

Brother Junior Warden, look well to the South!

CHAPTER VIII
THE CHAPLAIN'S PLACE

In a Masonic lodge, the thoughtful observer discovers that nearly every object about him has a meaning. And here is the point at which symbolism comes into the picture. During the Work, attention is directed to various symbols about the lodge room. Even the location of each officer has a meaning.

This chapter is designed to direct the reader's attention to the Chaplain, to his place and duties, especially in light of the symbolic meetings of the office. Upon entering a lodge, one is struck with the significance of the Chaplain's place — at the left of the Master in the East. Symbolized here are leadership and spirituality, side by side. Here it symbolized that he who leads must lean on things spiritual if he would build that which will endure. Considering the Chaplain's place in the lodge, we see why he must be in his proper Place — at the left of the Master in the East.

Too often, I see a Chaplain seated on the sideline. As a matter of humility, perhaps this may be commended, but there are times when humility is not a virtue, and this is one of them. I have often seen a Chaplain seated in the Marshal's chair, which is also wrong. The Chaplain's place is in the East, even as Solomon, we are told, placed at his side the High Priest so that the mighty and wise King might benefit from spiritual advice.

Now let us consider the Chaplain's work — and by that, I have in mind the part that he plays during the ritualistic work and in the various forms and ceremonies.

The Chaplain's chief task is to lead the devotions of the lodge. The prayers at the opening and the closing of the lodge, and those repeated from time to time during the Work, have as much a place in the scheme of things as any other detail of the ritual.

I have known Masters so derelict in their conception of duty as to permit their lodges to be opened and closed without prayer. For a Worshipful Master to disregard the spiritual side of Masonry is bound to be disruptive, sooner or later, to the harmony in the lodge. And it must be apparent that no human institution can live up to its highest possible ideals and ignore the spiritual things. Many have tried and are still trying, but the effort will sooner or later be marked by failure. We must not, we dare not, neglect the spiritual aspects of life. All of which emphasize the significance of the Chaplain's prominent place before the brethren and the importance of his duties.

We should now glance at the ritualistic side of the Chaplain's work. In the opening and closing of the lodge, certain prayers are used. The prayers are contained in most standard Monitors and are to be used as they appear — unless the Chaplain is sufficiently gifted to improve on them. I have heard of many attempts at improvement, but only once or twice has the effort proved a success. In these prayers, as in all of our Work, the theme, or motif (call it what you choose), is "Harmony." Analyze these prayers. For example:

> "Grant that the sublime principles of Freemasonry may so subdue every discordant passion within us, so harmonize and enrich our hearts with Thine own love and goodness, that the lodge at this time may humbly reflect that order and beauty which reign forever before Thy Throne."

Again, at the closing of the lodge, observe this beautiful petition to the Great Architect:

"Subdue every discordant passion within us and enable us to love one another in the bonds of union and friendship."

And here I also say, observe how impressively the theme of harmony is woven throughout the passage. Like any profound musical selection, any book worthwhile, any master painting — in short, like any great work of art, these prayers have a quality that makes them live. Their prose is inspired; in its rhythm is a majesty that moves us mightily and with a striking sincerity of appeal.

As is true everywhere in our Ritual, the English of these prayers is cartelized by a careful smoothness, a ruggedness, and a fixity of purpose, to be found in a few of the masterpieces of composition. With it, in the quality of incisiveness that only sincerity can lend. Brother Chaplain, use them — unless you are so exceptionally gifted as to be able to improve upon them!

In light of these considerations, is it cause for wonder that we are appalled as we listen to some of the prayers offered to the Supreme Architect? Some time ago, I had the chance to be present at the opening of a lodge. The Chaplain stepped to the altar for the opening prayer. I was amazed at the poor man's fearful and wonderful conception of life as I listened. He prayed to the good Lord to give us the strength to withstand the trials and tribulations of this "vale of tears," particularly the trial of our daily occupation.

Perhaps he meant well. I don't know. But Heaven help the man who looks with repugnance upon the fact that he is obliged to work, and God bless the man who can put his feet out upon the floor in the morning, and he, like Saint Paul, has a race to run. Moreover, it may be a personal feeling, but the thread bears allusion to life as a *vale of tears* never fails to leave me cold. It involves a miserable philosophy of living. The Master who drew our designs never intended us to take so abject an attitude toward anything of His providing.

Many times, too, I have observed Chaplains give prayers from the sidelines. This practice lacks proper dignity and fails utterly to achieve impressiveness. It encourages an idea that prayer is not particularly important, whereas, if the Chaplain is in his proper place, his appeal for divine guidance is elevated to the high standard to which it belongs.

These prayers and the Scripture passages I shall presently allude to should be memorized. The passage, however, is to be read or sung by the Chaplain; they are to be rendered from the side of the alter nearest the Senior Warden and with the Chaplain facing the East.

Since the Holy Bible is in the center of the room, the focal point of the attention of all, it is fitting that the Chaplain do his work here as a matter of association if for no other reason. Around the spiritual should our lives revolve. Symbolically the lodge represents life, "from the rising of the sun to the going down of the same," wherefore it is appropriate that that which relates to the spiritual in our work be performed in the center of the room.

In light of these considerations, is it to be wondered if we are dismayed at the spectacle of a Master opening his lodge without prayer? Can one conceive a Master so lacking in the sense of the fitness of things as to permit his brethren to leave without prayer?

CHAPTER IX
THE TREASURER

Too often, the Treasurer is one of the unsung heroes of the lodge. He occupies one of the two desks next to the Worshipful Master, but what does he really do? His station may be one of the most undervalued and misunderstood positions.

In most jurisdictions, the Treasurer's duties are similar to:

"To receive and receipt for all monies from the Secretary, keep a correct account of the same and pay them out by order of the Worshipful Master and the consent of the lodge."

Sounds rather straightforward and uncomplicated, right? Think again. The primary responsibility of the Treasurer is the financial affairs of the lodge. That's no small or unimportant task. One very quick way for a lodge to cease to exist is for the funds of the lodge to disappear. At the very least, it should require one who is well-organized and detail-oriented. No lodge needs a disorganized mess for its financial records.

A successful lodge is fully rounded, with all of the officers performing their duties as diligently as possible. Creativity cannot be underestimated as a key feature of a successful lodge. The Treasurer's duties may be spelled out in the most basic sense, but the creative Treasurer will provide additional service to the lodge. A responsible Treasurer will consistently monitor and evaluate the funds and investments of the lodge. He will also monitor the market trends so that he will be aware if any investments are yielding the best returns for the lodge. If the Treasurer learns that one investment is not proving best for the lodge, he will know to advise that the lodge move its funds or investments elsewhere.

The Treasurer can often work hand in hand with the Secretary to ensure that the lodge gets the most for its money. Most lodges employ vendors' services for items such as food, flowers, greeting cards, and so on. Not all vendors provide the best services or prices. A lodge can determine if it is getting the most for its money by evaluating the vendors.

It is always best to have a Treasurer with accounting experience, but even when a lodge has no member with such experience, it is far from a hopeless situation. Any conscientious and dedicated member can make good use of the many accounting programs available on a computer. Most of these programs are user-friendly and require only the desire to do the job correctly.

The Treasurer handles the money of the lodge. It is a most responsible job and deserves the full attention of the Treasurer and the lodge. With the support of the lodge and the diligent, dedicated effort of the Treasurer, a lodge with even a modest income can improve its financial position.

CHAPTER X
THE SECRETARY

So clearly does the ritual define the duty of each officer that one has only to scan the spoken word for a correct understanding of the several Stations and Places. In the ritual, the language is clearly stated and with a clear simplicity of expression that allows for no misunderstanding. There is no excuse for laxity on the ground of misunderstanding, no excuse for an assumption of authority that is not the right or the prerogative of the chair in question.

This chapter concerns the Secretary of the lodge along with some experience with and considerable observation of, Secretaries whom I have met during the past years. By far, the great majority have been splendid officers. Their books have been models of neatness and legibility. They are prompt in the performance of every duty. In some cases, I have discovered evidence of literary ability to add to the "fair record" required, and the minutes of one man formed a record that was of tremendous help to a brother who, later on, was busied in writing a history of the lodge.

Nor is there any reason why pride in a lodge's history not be expressed. Some lodges not only read the minutes of the last Communication but also go back over the minutes of ten or twenty years and read them. Then, we appreciate that completeness that takes us back to other times and gives us a complete and clear picture of the events occurring in an early day. It is educational.

But there is a very important thing that a good Secretary must do to serve his brethren. It is mentioned in the recital of his duty in the opening of the lodge. Let's look at it — and as it is monitorial, I may quote:

> "To observe the proceedings of the lodge, make a fair record of all things proper to be written, receive all money due the lodge, pay the same to the Treasurer, and perform such other duties as may be prescribed by the Constitutions of the Grand lodge."

For simplicity and directness, this bit of ritual will be about the same in any lodge. No superfluous word — a smoothness of diction — a statement of all that is to be done! But the second word is, to my mind, the most important of the statement: "OBSERVE"! His is not to dictate to the Master and the Wardens but to "observe" what is going on and, having observed, to make a fair record of those things pertaining to the lodge's business that are "proper to be written." And there is a large order.

Words mean little unless they are considered in the light of their interpretation, and no interpretation of the word "observe" can, by any stretch of the imagination, be considered as giving the Secretary license to attempt to give orders to the Worshipful Master. This is a sheer presumption. Years of service and knowledge of good Masonic practice do not give any brother dictatorial powers. Any Secretary who so interprets his work as to include the right to tell the Master how to run his lodge is heading, sooner or later, to a failure. His business is that of an observer, and a recorder of those things he observes, provided they are proper to be written.

I am fond of interpreting an officer's work in the light of his duty as recited in the ritual. Therein is completeness, free from overstatement. The diction is incisive, calculated to bite into the mind. In this respect, the ritual of Craft Masonry is unique in that it possesses those qualities of diction that impress the mind of the hearer, both with the beauty of the English and the lessons it teaches.

And may I comment on one word that represents a desirable quality for all Secretaries: "Promptness"! Nothing is more aggravating to one with business-like tendencies than to be held up by un-business-like practices on the part of one given to procrastination and tardiness. Onto the desk of the Secretary passes the lodge's business. The Secretary may well be called the businessman of the lodge, and promptness is one of the qualities of a successful businessman and is one which the Secretary of a lodge particularly should exemplify. The phrase, "To make a full and accurate return," stresses the need for accuracy in the Secretary's work. It has been my observation that in those cases where the lodge records disagree with those in the Grand Secretary's office concerning such matters as the number of members, nearly always, the error has been made by the lodge Secretary.

To assist the Secretary (like the Treasurer) in some of his duties, a good number of computer programs and software have been developed which may assist him — some of these wholly Masonic in design. The internet can provide a library of information on how the Secretary may improve and streamline the performance of his duties. It only requires the desire to make the most of what is available.

"Make a Fair Record"! This, many times, is a large order. And always, it is enough of a task to give the conscientious Brother elected to the Office an opportunity to serve his lodge in a manner that will call for the best in him. And in properly performing his task, he will grow immeasurably in spiritual and intellectual stature.

CHAPTER XI
"BROTHER SENIOR DEACON"

Of all the officers of their lodge, none have a finer opportunity to make his lodge a place where the warm spirit of hospitality is exemplified than does the Senior Deacon. He is often called the "Top Sergeant" of the lodge. Perhaps this is why the emblem upon his staff and apron is the blazing sun. To warmly welcome the visiting brethren! Through him, the lodge displays the crowning glory of the home — the spirit of hospitality! The lodge should be where Brotherly love abides and where kindly courtesy and consideration shine forth as the sun at meridian, the glory and beauty of the day. The courtesy is extended not only to visitors but to candidates as well!

In the ceremony of installation, the Master of Ceremonies is told that he "as a proxy for the Senior Deacon is to see that candidates are duly and truly prepared." Consideration and courtesy should be sensed by every candidate, and in a measure, the Senior Deacon is responsible for this because the Master of Ceremonies acts for him. His influence as the head of the committee for welcoming should, therefore, be felt when a man first steps into the preparation room.

Again, most of us have been in lodges where icicles seem to hang from the chandeliers. Maybe, one or two members would greet a visitor. All seemed indifferent.

They didn't mean to make you feel ill at ease; they simply had the bad habit of appearing inhospitable. They probably were never taught better. And probably the lodge was entirely unconscious of having this attitude.

The Senior Deacon has the opportunity to make his lodge a shining place of welcome to the visitor, who, having come once, will want to come again.

Just run over the Senior Deacon's duty in your mind and observe that this matter of welcoming visiting brethren comes before the attending of candidates. How splendidly can he serve his lodge by thus exemplifying the true spirit of the Craft!

It would seem clear, then, that the Senior Deacon's first care is that of being hospitable. Now let us consider that part of his work involves the receiving and conducting of candidates. You remember how having assured the Worshipful Master of the proper performance of his duty by the Master of Ceremonies, he receives the candidate. The first words the candidate hears in the lodge are from the Senior Deacon. A quiet, distinct manner of expression, an effort to bring out the great lessons of the ritual at this point, will not only create a tremendous impression on the mind of the candidate but also will bring home to his consciousness the great truths therein contained.

Our attitude toward candidates should be one of kind consideration. Their treatment in the preparation room should reaffirm this thought. Started in the mind and continued in the lodge, we have every opportunity of welding our new members to the Craft with lasting bonds.

The Floor-work of the degree is not difficult. The Senior Deacon should be thoroughly familiar with it. It is done under his direction. He has the assistance of a Marshal. The orderly conduct of the procession is important.

Excepting the Worshipful Master, the Senior Deacon has more of the ritual to render than any other officer. He has dialogues while conferring a degree with nearly every officer in the lodge. Of necessity, therefore, he should be as familiar with the Work of his brother officers as with his own so that the Work may go smoothly. The Master and the Wardens unconsciously lean on a good Senior Deacon.

Let him forget words, make a misstep, attempt to carry on with a faulty knowledge of his work, and the entire degree conferral falters.

Now let me say something about how the Senior Deacon's work is rendered. If there is one thing that will help the officers of lodges to make the work impressive, it is proper articulation. We should not mumble and jumble in a rushed manner until it is extremely difficult to understand what is being said. Clear speech is entirely a matter of habit. Get in that habit, Brother Senior Deacon, so all you say may be intelligible to every brother present. A Senior Deacon who rattles through his work with no expression fails to drive home the impressive lessons to be taught.

No two Senior Deacons are precisely alike. Each has his peculiarities. I remember one lodge meeting where the Senior Deacon was everything one would expect, but his suit was somewhat worn and tattered. He knew his ritual and the floor-work; he was dignified, calm, self-possessed. He bore out the truth of the statement that the internal and not the external qualifications recommend a man to Masons. One forgot the manner of his dress in admiration of the man and Mason.

One of the best Senior Deacons I ever met was a brother of humble attainments regarding educational advantages. His work had been taught to him by his brethren and by word of mouth. His mind was like a strip of blotting paper — it "soaked up" the ritual.

If he made an error, one correction was all that was necessary on that particular point. He did not make the same mistake twice. Moreover, he required very little correcting. His work was almost perfect. Never have I met a man more anxious to be corrected or more grateful for being told what was right.

We have all kinds — the proud, the humble, the careful, the careless, those who are rash, and some who are conceited. But, I have yet to meet one who willfully makes errors. All are "Architects of Faith Working in these halls of Time!"

CHAPTER XII
THE JUNIOR DEACON

This chapter is not written with a thought in mind merely for the brethren who today occupy the important office of Junior Deacon. It is written as well for the other thousands who will come after them and for that still greater body of brothers who, though they will never enter the line, enjoy the ritualistic work of the lodge directly in proportion as they comprehend and understand the function of each officer taking part in the work. Add to this those brethren who have already seen service in this and other stations of the lodge, and just about everybody is included in the audience, which I envisage for these paragraphs.

First, let us run over in our minds the duty of the Junior Deacon as he relates and analyzes it. It is four-fold:

1. to carry messages
2. to attend to alarms
3. to report the same
4. to see that the lodge is duly tiled

Now for the first duty — to carry messages. The Senior Deacon, the "Top Sergeant" of the lodge, carries orders. The Junior Deacon carries messages. He is an aide to the Senior Warren, not only in this respect but also in tyling the lodge. We shall consider this aspect later. The two Deacons are proxies for the Master and Wardens. We read in the installation ceremony found in many Standard Monitors that,

"... it is your duty to attend on the Master and Wardens, to act as their proxies in the active duties of the lodge, such as the reception of candidates and the introduction and accommodation of visitors."

A little contemplation will bring to mind a number of places where the Deacons act as proxies.

For the second duty, the Junior Deacon attends all alarms at the outer door and reports them to the Worshipful Master. Samuel Pritchard's 1760 classic *Three Distinct Knocks* should explain how a proper alarm should be given. An alarm is neither random in the number of knocks nor ill-timed or varying in audio levels. The alarm should not be light taps nor attempts to break down the door. It is three distinct knocks. The Junior Deacon should attend the alarm similarly — as prescribed by ritual. Over the years, I have seen many creative methods of giving alarms — all incorrect. I've seen taps given so lightly that the lodge membership could barely hear it, I've seen cute rhythmic patterns worked out between the Tyler and Junior Deacon (having nothing to do with Masonry), I've seen wholly random knocks as if someone was knocking on the door of a home and I have even seen no alarms whatsoever with only the Tyler or Junior Deacon opening the door when they felt it was needed.

Our Junior Deacons and Tylers should also note that no part of their work will ever be repeated at low breath. Only one portion of our secret work is communicated that way, which is not given at the outer door. Each Brother has a right to hear every word of every dialogue between these two officers. Certainly, whispers are not easily distinguishable in the more remote corners of the lodge.

The Worshipful Master should instruct the Tyler and Junior Deacon never to permit brethren to enter through the

Inner Door. Brethren are admitted through the Inner Door only on the order of the Master of the lodge.

Let me say that the Junior Deacon and the Tyler should require brethren to leave the smokes outside the lodge. A Masonic lodge is not a social club. The odor of stale tobacco smoke is simply out of place, with the Holy Bible on the altar in the center of the lodge. The lodge is the gathering place for a group of dignified individuals assembled for a constructive solemn business — the building of character.

In the tyling of the lodge, the Junior Deacon plays an important part as a proxy of the Senior Deacon. He first ascertains and then reports to the West (in some jurisdictions) that all present are Master Masons. And I would like to suggest to the Junior Deacon and Tyler that before the lodge opens, and during refreshment, they remain at the outer door, that those who would enter, but for whom neither can vouch, be caused to remain outside until properly vouched for or examined. This procedure will save much time later on.

In the heyday of U.S. Masonry (the 1950s & 60's), it was common for someone wishing to work his way through the chairs to wait (while providing dedicated service) a number of years before reaching the Junior Deacon's station. Many lodges could have 4 to 6 Stewards ahead of him. Today, this is often not the case. Unfortunately, the Junior Deacon's station is either the very first station worked by someone or, if they prove themselves as having some ability, are quickly advanced to the Senior Deacon's station. The impression is given that the Junior Deacon's station is an "unimportant" position and is often a revolving door station with the office filled each meeting by a different Past Master. Such activity is a disservice to the station and the whole lodge.

Masonry teaches us that only those structures possessing a solid foundation are of true value. The Junior Deacon's station is one of the foundational stations. While he may not have as many lines of ritual to recite, the proper performance of his duties is essential to a successful lodge. The wise Worshipful Master will be certain that the one holding this important station is well-trained, responsible, and dedicated to the lodge and properly performing his duties.

CHAPTER XIII
THE MASTER OF CEREMONIES

Eugene Covill, the candidate, and Ed Westbrook, the Tyler, sat in the ante-room of Finger Lakes Lodge. Nearly half an hour ago, the Junior Deacon had informed Ed that the lodge was open on the third degree of Masonry. At times a low-voiced conversation passed between the two men, but for the most part, Gene was with his thoughts. He had been notified to be present to receive the First Degree. He was happy, and soon he would realize his fondest hope of being made a Mason.

He remembered his grandfather, a man of sturdy New England stock, to whom his father had often pointed with pride "as an upright man and Mason." To Gene, he had been the living embodiment of such a man. When he was a little boy, there was born in Gene's heart a great desire to know more about this Masonry of which he heard so much but which he knew so little. And now tonight...

Before the lodge meeting started, he had been greeted by Frank Vogt, the Worshipful Master, Ed Pickard, the Senior Warden, and Floyd Holmes, the Junior Warden, as well as the rest of the brethren. He was impressed by their welcome and the spirit of kind hospitality that pervaded the room. At no time was the conversation directed into channels calculated to rouse his fear or concern. No jokes were told at his expense. Apparently, all present tried to give him a beneficial impression of our ancient institution.

While they were thus engaged in their thoughts, two lodge officers appeared. He followed them into the preparation room, where the Worshipful Master awaited him.

Here his mind was further prepared for what was to follow. The quiet demeanor of the three men gave him confidence, as the words of the Master assured him that "Freemasonry is far removed from all that is trivial, selfish, and ungodly. . ." The usual questions were answered, and the Master returned to the lodge room.

The quiet, respectful demeanor of the three officers in the preparation room, together with the absence of useless frivolity and crude jokes, had made a lasting impression on the mind of this candidate for Masonry. And this was as it should be. Nothing should be left undone to convey to the mind of the candidate the seriousness of the step he is about to take. The demeanor of the brethren he meets, the absence of a spirit of levity and skylarking in the ante-room, as well as in the preparation room, will go far toward laying a foundation on which will rest the structure into which his mind perfectly fits as a "Living Stone."

To further this aim, a Monitor wisely states that,

> "When the candidate for initiation shall have entered the preparation room, the Master of the lodge or some other officer or member shall, by direction of the Worshipful Master, repair thither and may address him as follows."

And the address which does follow is too often greatly neglected. To read it in a stumbling, halting fashion robs it of its beauty and must fail utterly to impress the candidate with the truths it contains.

And what of the Inner Door directly leading from the Preparation Room to the mysteries beyond? This candidate for Masonry must pass through it. Yet, no Tyler sits outside; no

Junior Deacon guards its portals from within. It is unique in this respect, as no other door is like it. The entire lodge guards it, each member of which holds that mystic key, the ballot in their hand.

I well remember a lodge I once visited where no preparation room existed. When questioned about the missing room, the lodge brother said, "We are obliged to use the anti-room as a preparation room because the arrangement of these rooms, which we rent, leaves no space for one." I hope no such condition exists today, but if it does exist, the Worshipful Master should require his brethren to remain outside of the ante-room while candidates are here prepared.

That night, as on other nights, no privacy was afforded the candidate, and it seemed to us that the lodge failed utterly to impress him with the solemnity of the occasion. Instead of being made to realize that he was to be a child groping his way in darkness for light to illuminate his pathway, the candidate must have gained the impression that it was just another case of "joining." No feeling of earnestness or purpose permeated the atmosphere. Candidates were received into the lodge with no conception of the importance of their steps. Let me say, in passing, that this condition has been remedied in that lodge. The ante-room has been remodeled at comparatively little expense, while a preparation room has been provided that is both comfortable and commodious.

A similar situation existed in another lodge. Here portable screens had been used to provide a semblance of seclusion in the preparation room — a half-hearted attempt at privacy. Every effort of the Master of Ceremonies and the Master to lend an air of dignity to the occasion was lost. Nothing could offset the confusion of talk and laughter of the brethren during the period of refreshment. It is safe to say that candidates prepared under these conditions were only a little better off than if no screens at all had been provided.

These were extreme cases, but they are examples of neglectfulness and thoughtlessness against which every lodge should guard. The thought of preparing candidates under such conditions is intolerable and should not be acceptable to any lodge. No matter how well the degree may be conferred, an irremovable scar is left on the minds of the initiates, which time seldom removes.

The doors leading into the preparation room should be locked from the inside (to cause the candidate no concern) while candidates are being prepared. This will prevent useless running to and fro by the brethren of the lodge unless other means are provided for privacy. No matter how luxurious the preparation room may be (and luxury is not necessary here), the desired effect is lost unless the unmindful are kept out. This room should be quiet in its appointments, devoted to a certain purpose only, and privacy should be maintained. No one should be permitted here except those whose duty requires their presence. Then, too, I would see that all ritualistic garb was such as would not offend the finer sensibilities of any candidate. There is no excuse for musty, damp, or soiled garments. Launder all items that need it!

Proper mental preparation and correct ritualistic preparation — that is the point! Eugene Covill had been properly prepared. It is safe to say he went "out from that evening's ceremonies a loyal Mason, a worthy brother, an apprentice entered upon a new field of labor, with a new sense of duty, and bound by a solemn vow ever to walk and act uprightly, and speak His name reverently before whom all Masons should humbly, reverently end devoutly bow."

CHAPTER XIV
SCRIPTURE LESSON FIRST AND SECOND DEGREE

I have always been impressed with the wide variety of interests shown by brethren in things Masonic. In three different directions, I have observed them to be practically absorbed.

For one thing, Masons are interested in one another. They like to be told about the conditions the other brothers live under. In other words, they respond to the human side of Masonry.

In the second place, Masons are interested in the Grand Lodge Constitutions and Laws. Worshipful Masters have succeeded in simply reading sections from their Grand Lodge Constitutions in the lodge. I know of one lodge which invited the District Deputy Grand Master to a particular meeting where various Grand Lodge laws were read, followed by a question and answer session by the District Deputy. It was a most successful meeting.

And, finally, a lively interest is shown in the allegory of our Scripture readings, particularly that impressive picture of old age given in Ecclesiastes 12:1-7, Our Scripture lesson in the Third Degree. Of equal interest, though perhaps less picturesque, is the interpretation of the Scripture lessons for the First and Second Degrees, a subject that I want to look into for a few moments.

Responding to many demands for an explanation of this allegory, I venture the following suggestions, based for the greater part on Cooke's *Commentary on the Old Testament*. Much of it is my own, the result of much thought.

Now before we can appreciate, or even understand, the hidden meaning of these portions of Scripture, we must know the meaning and the application of two words, "symbolism" and "allegory." I suggest that we look rather carefully at these two terms. And first to the word "symbol." Webster defines a symbol as a visible sign of an idea or quality of another object. "The lion is a symbol of courage," for example.

While we are all familiar with the use of symbols, we can often fail to realize the extent to which symbolism enters into our everyday lives. In learning to speak, a child utters sounds that gradually take on the semblance of words. And since words are symbols of ideas or objects, a child learning to read is learning to use symbols.

We visit an auto parts store and ask the clerk to give us a quart of oil. In this negotiation, we employ symbolism because "quart" symbolizes a definite quantity we wish to purchase. The same principle holds in purchasing five pounds of sugar at the grocer's or specifying the length of our trousers in inches.

All through life, we use symbols. The engineer in designing a roof truss uses the word "pounds" to symbolize the load the structure is to carry. We are all familiar with the Cross of Christ, the six-pointed star of David, the plumb, the square, the level, the twenty-four-inch gauge, and the common gavel. We are also aware that the Bible in the center of the lodge room symbolizes Light radiating in all directions. The letter "G" in the East, the Master's gavel, and the ashlars are of deepest significance to him, who best understands the wealth of meaning in the word "symbolism."

Masons are well acquainted with symbolism. Masonically, we have been brought up on it and never are appalled just because the word is unusual, though frequent enough in its applications.

When we come to the word "allegory," however, here is something with which we may be somewhat unfamiliar. The Greek word from which it comes means describing one thing under the image of another. Or, if we want to alter this definition, we may say that it is a definition of one thing in terms of something else. Webster's dictionary defines "allegory" as "a representation by a figurative story of something metaphorically suggested, but not expressly stated."

The first seven verses of the twelfth chapter of Ecclesiastes are an allegory that may be interpreted in more than one way. The interpretation given later is one, while some prefer its interpretation as a storm in Palestine. One may take his choice.

In this particular bit of Scripture, the words "old age" are not mentioned, yet, as you will see, it is a perfect image of old death, decay of the physical body, and the transfer of the soul to life everlasting. And yet none of these things are mentioned in so many words. All is left to the reader's imagination, for which reason, if we are to get the rich lessons from allegory and symbols, we will need an active imagination.

With a good comprehension of symbolism and allegory, any Mason will find his Masonic life infinitely richer in all its realms. He will see new beauties in our teachings and history that he may have never understood. Freemasonry is defined as "a system of morals, illustrated by symbols, and veiled in allegory." That is a splendid definition, even though "symbolism" and "allegory" often seem like twelve-pound words.

Let us look at that portion of the Scriptures appointed for the First Degree and discover why it is used for that particular portion of our Work. David wrote it. You see, David was a practical man with no illusions about life or people. He realized what many of his people did not, and many of us fail to realize today, that men should live together in harmony. Harmony is the theme and motif of this one-hundred-and-thirty-third Psalm. For unity is harmony. The very first Scripture lesson heard by a candidate in a lodge room is the lesson of "harmony," written by David, the father of Solomon:

"Behold, how good and how pleasant it is for brethren to dwell together in unity! It is like the precious ointment upon the head, then ran down upon the beard, even Aaron's beard: that went down to the skirts of his garments. As the dew of Hermon, and as the dew that descended upon the mountains of Zion; for there the Lord commanded the blessing, even life forevermore."

Let us look at a few features of this Psalm. David commences it with the word "Behold," a word with a peculiar usage in the Scriptures. The writer in Hebrew in the Old Testament and Greek in the New often used the word to direct attention emphatically upon something important to follow. The effect was much the same as that of "Attention!" given a company of soldiers by its commanding officer — from positions of ease, the soldiers became alert, and alert should be the mind upon confronting this word "Behold." David was so impressed with the importance of harmony among men that he commenced this chapter on harmony with the word.

"The precious ointment poured upon the head of Aaron flowing over his beard and clothing consecrated the man and his vestments and united

64

them as one body filling all space around with a delightful fragrance. Concord of brethren united in one will and living as brethren is similarly excellent and previous, diffusing all around a delightful satisfaction; and suggesting to those who witness it, a vision of peace, love, sympathy, and brotherly love ever-extending."

So says Clarke in his Commentary on this Psalm. Clarke says, too, that the "skirts" of the clothing is the upper edge, or border, terminating the robe and girding the neck or perhaps the lower edge or rim, terminating the robe below the waist. "Concord" is like the dew of Hermon: it falls gently, copiously, imperceptibly, watering the Land of Promise.

The power of the above lines shine in the second and third verses. It becomes apparent only when we realize the impossibility of causing the mixing of oil and water. But the Psalmist does it spiritually! For some brethren to attempt to dwell together in unity might seem as impossible as mixing oil and water, wherefore how gentle and fine is the influence when those of opposing temperaments can adjust themselves to one another. The thought of harmony, or unity, runs like a stream of light, like a thread of gold, through all our rituals. What finer portion of Scripture could have been selected for the First Degree than this one hundred and thirty-third Psalm?

In the Second Degree, the portion of Scripture appointed to be read, recited, or sung at the end of the perambulation is the seventh and eighth verses of the seventh chapter of the book of Amos. It is a bit of Scripture particularly adapted to the Second Degree, for the plumb-line is mentioned. The plumb line is an important part of a plumb, and the plumb is one of the working tools of Fellowcraft.

"Thus, you showed me; behold, the Lord stood upon a wall made by a plumb-line, with a plumb-line in His hand. And the Lord said unto me, 'Amos, what seest thou?' And I said, 'a plumb-line.' Then said the Lord, 'Behold, I will set in plumb-line in the midst of my people Israel: I will not again pass by them anymore.'"

Observe that the word "Behold" is used twice, and a significant statement follows each occasion. It has always seemed to me that the word "wall" is, but an allegory of a man's life built four square and true by the square of virtue, the plumb of the uprightness of character, and the plumb line of good judgment. The plumb is an implement of the uprightness of character, and to me, the plumb-line is a symbol of good judgment, that very necessary quality in the mind of man.

A man may possess money, but he cannot use it wisely without judgment. He may be brilliant, yet if he has no judgment, his wisdom is much less beneficial to himself or others.

The man of wisdom is wise because knowledge does not become knowledge until it is passed on to the minds of others, or, as the poet Browning so aptly expressed it, "when we lend our minds." Only in the Second Degree is the word "judgment" used, and those familiar with their ritual remember that portion of the Work.

And I repeat, in closing, that it would have been difficult to choose a lovelier or a more apt bit of scripture for the Second Degree than the seventh and eighth verses of the seventh chapter of the book of Amos.

CHAPTER XV
"IN THE DAYS OF THY YOUTH"

"Remember now thy Creator in the days of thy youth, while the evil days come not, nor the years draw nigh when thou shalt say, I have no pleasure in them. . ."

This verse is a part of the preceding chapter, and unfortunately, interruption by our system of chapter and verse division breaks. The man who knocks at our inner door in the Third Degree, as far as his Masonic life is concerned, is not a youth, but we still remind him of the importance of remembering his Creator, that his old age may not be a season of the dreariness. Thus, he may show his gratitude to God. It is brought directly to our attention that the wisdom of acquiring while we are young, the habit of the Godly life before the evil days, the season of old age, shall come upon us.

"While the sun, or the light, or the moon, or the stars, be not darkened, nor the clouds return after the rain. . . ."

If we read the word "while" as "before," and the words "or" and "nor" as "and," the meaning of this passage becomes suddenly apparent. The darkening of the lights of Heaven points to a time of affliction and sadness, and we hear an address to a youth who should be made vividly aware of old age. In other words, the writer alludes to a heaviness of spirit that frequently accompanies age.

"In the day when the keepers of the house shall tremble, and strong men shall bow themselves, and

the grinders cease because there are few, and those
that look out of windows be darkened..."

It is not unusual to hear the body describe as a tent, or a
house, in which dwells the spirit of man. The keepers of the
house are the knees and the hand, which, through weakness,
tremble in old age. The strong men are the vertebrae in the
back, and in old age, the back becomes bent. The grinders are
the teeth; in their advanced years, people lose their teeth —
hence "the grinders cease because they are few." "Those that
look out of the window be darkened" alludes to the eyes.
Cooke says that the window was the frequent resource of the
women in the Oriental house, and here the windows represent
the eyes, dim in old age.

"And the doors shall be shut in the streets when
the sound of the grinding is low, and he shall rise at
the voice of the birds, and all the daughters of music
shall be brought low. . . "

Here we look at the house from the outside. The doors
speak to us of deafness. The sounds of grinding show that
there is no sound coming out of the house to tell of life within.
Because they live so much to themselves, old people have less
in common with the rising generation than the young. If we
seek a counterpart to the doors in the sound of the grinding in
the body, we may take them as figures of speech, alluding to
the lips and the ears because the door to the house is
sometimes taken as the lips. "The sound of the grinding is
low" — an allusion to deafness.

"He shall rise at the voice of the bird" — here, the allegory
of the house ends. We may interpret the statement in this
manner: it alludes to the master of a house as an old man

awakening early at the first sound of morning, based on the fact that elderly people frequently do not sleep well.

"The daughters of music shall be brought low" — again, an allusion to deafness because the music sounds faintly in the ears of old age. And then, too, on the day of death, the work of the household is hushed; the sounds of an ordinary occupation are unheard.

> "Also, when they shall be afraid of that which is high, and fears shall be in the way, and the almond tree shall flourish, and the grasshopper shall be a burden, and desire shall fail; because man goeth to his long home, and the mourners go about the streets..."

Old age is inclined to timidity, and "high" is used elsewhere in scriptures to denote proud, powerful people from whom an old person with the timidity of age might shrink. The almond tree alludes to the hair; in bloom, the almond tree is white, the blossoms completely covering the tree. Again, we have a beautiful allusion to an outstanding characteristic of age. Old people are easily troubled; their means of physical and intellectual defense has declined in power. Accordingly, grasshoppers are used here to characterize the little troubles that fret and worry the aged and that younger people can easily thrust aside. The locust is a highly active insect, and the aged, burdened with stiffness of joints and heaviness, often resent the physical and mental agility of the young.

The phrase, "and desire shall fail," alludes to the caperberry, which, in Oriental countries, was eaten as a stimulus to the appetite, but which fails to help one whose powers are exhausted.

The "long home" has reference to man's "eternal house," as the passage would be translated, and to his place in the next world.

"Mourners go about the streets" — it was the custom for a bereaved family to employ singing women, who went about the streets mourning the loss of one who had died, whence the phrase alludes to the day of death.

"Or ever the silver cord be loosed, or the golden bowl be broken, or the pitcher be broken at the fountain, or the wheel be broken at the cistern..."

The breaking of a lamp here represents death because the silver cord was that by which the household lamp was suspended from the ceiling. The lamp represents life, and when the silver cord is broken, the lamp is dashed into pieces, and the light is extinguished. The golden bowl alludes to the reservoir of oil used in the lamp, which also is broken in the fall.

The pitcher in ancient times was used to bring water from the spring. No longer on the day of death is the substance of water needed, and the pitcher is broken. The wheel let down into the cistern, brings water from the depths, but on the day of death, it is no longer needed and therefore is broken.

I would like to put a somewhat different interpretation of this passage. I like to think of the silver cord as the spinal cord, which after death, disintegrates. To me, the golden bowl represents the skull, the broken pitcher, the heart, which no longer functions, and the broken wheel, those who are engaged in the ordinary occupations of daily life but who cease on the day of death.

"Then shall the dust return to the earth as it was, and the spirit shall return unto God who gave it."

The figure of the dust returning to the earth alludes to the complete disintegration and darkness of this, our earthly tabernacle. Here is the last touch, a consummate description — rather depressing but nonetheless true. And its glory and comfort are that dramatic finale, that shout of triumph, that comes like a great "Amen."

"The spirit shall return unto God who gave it!"

CHAPTER XVI
THIRD DEGREE

Even to a casual observer, it would seem that many of our lodges are getting far from a thorough understanding of the Second Section of the Third Degree. That is if one may judge by how this very important and beautiful portion of our work is sometimes conferred. I am thinking especially of the liberties we take with it — liberties we would not think of taking with any other part of the ritual. Here seems to come a kind of letdown; all of the meticulous care bestowed upon the work up to this point is thrown aside. In place of an accuracy upon which we pride ourselves in other parts of the ritual, carelessness creeps in. Let us look for a moment at some of the features of the Second Section. Most of the innovations referred to are due, I believe, to a lack of appreciation of the beauty of the Work there unfolded. Is there any Mason among us who does not feel the solemnity of the moment when for the first time, a candidate enters the lodge room? We are proud of the atmosphere of quiet dignity that prevails. We resent idle banter and jests at such a time. We are engaged in the serious business of bringing light to the minds of those who have placed themselves in our care for the time being. This is no place for jesting or idle banter.

Also, we will remember the manner of introducing the candidate to Masonry. We taught him the need of prayer before entering upon any great and important undertaking. We try the wells of his faith in Almighty God and clasp his mind in assurance that his faith is well founded.

How superb is such a commencement of his Masonic career? He proceeds in simple, childlike reverence; at every step, his feet are guided, and he fears no danger. Repeatedly, his mind is led to contemplate his Creator, the seriousness of moral obligations, and the truth that "no man liveth unto himself alone." All those who have gathered here are his brethren, and none there is whom he need fear.

Why do so many lodges disturb such a setting and compel their candidates to feel that all that has proceeded the Second Section of this degree may be but an illusion? Why do we often throw decorum to the winds with shouts of rowdy glee?

This section of the work contains passages as sublime as any found in the three degrees. In it are some of the most beautiful lessons of Masonry. Here is neither time nor place to indulge in crude comedy for the amusement of those on the sidelines, scenes to be greeted with peals of laughter. Undue roughness teaches absolutely nothing! Rather, it puts the candidate in a frame of mind exactly the opposite of that desired. We succeed only in shattering ideals we have striven previously to instill in his mind; because we have failed to comprehend the beauty of this section, it is lost to the candidate. No elaborate drama, with robes, trappings, and false whiskers, can equal the simple rendition of the work as Grand Lodge gives it to us. Frequently these adornments by their unfitness are an anachronism in themselves and simply add to the farce. Moreover, since few of us are actors, why try to act? If we find ourselves assigned to a part for which we are unsuited, using artificial means simply defeats our purpose.

If those lodges which set aside the regular work of the Second Section to use an elaboration of their own would put the same amount of time, energy, and thought into the ritual as Grand Lodge gives it, the work would take on new beauties, and a significance hitherto undreamed of. We would not permit anyone to tamper with the rest of the ritual for a moment. The situation, in large part, may be attributed to the fact that many lodges have their drama or form of rendition and arrogate to themselves the right to employ their language.

In the Second Section, a number of lessons are taught, lessons just as profound and beautiful as are to be found in any other portion of the work. Here are imparted the teachings of reverence and devotion to Almighty God. Here we are taught to rely upon Him in all we do and to invoke His aid before entering upon any great and important undertaking. This was taught in the First Degree. It is reemphasized here. Where, then, is room for humor?

And in the lesson of integrity, there is no place for mirth. Nor the lesson of wise men's unselfishness giving of themselves to a friend who comes to us with empty hands — helping him, even barefoot. Nor to the trust reposed in us when a brother comes to unburden a heart full of trouble, his is as sacred and secure in our breast as they were in his.

Is there a place, I repeat, for humor in this Section of the Third Degree? No, there is not. I do not, mind you, believe for a moment that the brother who chuckles in the most solemn passages of this solemn drama is incapable of feeling the tragedy set forth. This same brother would witness a performance of "Hamlet" and be stirred to the depths. But somehow, he misses the point when he attends a performance of our drama of the Third Degree — tragedy as profound, poignant, and universal in its appeal to the human soul as any other drama ever conceived. We must begin to see what we truly have in our degrees.

CHAPTER XVII
MASONIC ETIQUETTE

The charm of good manners! Like love, beauty, or music, it conquers where it stands, without force or argument, by its inherent shining and is its justification and reward. If we study etiquette, its code, and principle, it is because we have already won over to its claims and desire to shape ourselves to its appeal. Whether it be in the uses of politeness, gracious behavior, pleasing conduct, deportment, courtliness, or any other of those amenities of word and act by which a man is distinguished a gentleman among his fellows.

Like every circle in human society, Masonry has an etiquette of its own. Its foundations were laid by those Operative Masons to whom, being cathedral builders, architecture was more of an art than a trade and who learned refinement from their daily work. Its superstructure arose, generation by generation, through the decay of the cathedral building and the two centuries of transition. It continued to grow through the formative period of the Speculative Craft and has been refined; to the stage we have it by centuries of experience. In tens of thousands of Ancient Craft lodges, each of which has been itself a school of behavior, teaching the art of gentle manners more by practice than by precept.

In principle, Masonic etiquette belongs to the world of good manners. It is that code by which gentlemen the world over governs their conduct. But this principle with us is found to apply in two directions: on the one hand, it becomes a manifestation of respect for the Craft as a whole; on the other hand, it is a form of courtesy to the individual.

Freemasonry solicits no man to join it. It permits no man to make unauthorized innovations in its philosophy. Its candidates come of their own free will, and because they have heard good reports of its reputation, they have formed a favorable opinion of its work. And by all means, throughout its entire system, and through all its bodies and degrees, it is in every way secured that a Mason shall stand to it in an attitude of reverence and respect. Of that reverence and respect, etiquette is one of the forms.

From among the many who desire the honor of membership in its assemblies, it selects the few shown to have the necessary qualifications. Once admitted, they are endorsed with the seal of equal fellowship and placed in relation to the same rights, privileges, and duties as all others. No distinctions of wealth, station, rank, race, or creed are permitted. Among these members, it is a principal effort of the Craft to sustain unity and harmony, and it is one of the sovereign duties laid on every one of its officials. They are responsible for avoiding or prohibiting acts or conduct on the part of any that might militate against the Craft's being "a center of union." When this spirit and intent of the fraternity is itself to focus upon the individual, it takes the form of a sincere courtesy, and it is to give expression to this courtesy that much of Masonic etiquette exists.

There is a certain and clear beauty in the practice of Masonic etiquette. The Masonic life, as it is lived out in our assemblies, is a conscious work of art, with each and every part coordinated with every other and instinct with the feeling of the whole. If a man enters that system without preparation or forethought and trusting only his instincts, his manner will strike an awkward note, like a discord jangling across a strain of music. But if he has trained himself in his part and caught the spirit of the whole, the genius of Freemasonry will shine through his actions. It will express itself through him, just as, under other conditions, it expresses itself through ritual, symbol, law, philosophy, fellowship, and daily deeds. To have oneself thus become a part of a great and living whole is a satisfying pleasure nothing else can give, participation in the very life of beauty, appreciated as much by the beholders as by the actor. This ability to confer pleasure upon one's fellows when gathered in communication or ceremony is not the least of etiquette's rewards.

Harmony is the first law of the lodge as it is of heaven. Wherever discord enters, Freemasonry leaves. For one man to live in unity with another belongs to the very essence of our Royal Art; if unity is destroyed, fellowship becomes a pile of ashes, and the sun, moon, and stars of brotherhood are eclipsed by fog or storm. Since it is the nature of decorum to nurture and protect harmony, etiquette is a safeguard of the Craft, a certain insurance against many of those schisms and discords by which so much of the good work of a lodge may be destroyed in so short a time. "You talk about forms," exclaimed Goethe to a disciple, "as if a substance could be formless; neglect form and see how long you will have any substance!"

Our etiquette also guarantees equality in the Craft's treatment of its members. Imagine it to be destroyed by a stroke overnight, and Masons left to act out of prejudices or whims! The poor man would be snubbed by the rich, the timid overwhelmed by the brazen, the elected official would lord it over the layman, favoritism, class-consciousness, vanity, snobbery, and all the forms of an ugly secular worldliness would cut this way, and that across each lodge until Freemasonry would, at last, succumb to those very passions it now exists to control. Equality would be gone, that equality in which each man is treated with the same courtesy as every other; the sword would replace the Level among the Working Tools.

At the same time, and by the same token, Masonic etiquette possesses a utility, the full extent of which has often escaped notice. That utility consists in the power to enable many men of different abilities, and without rehearsal, to act in concert through elaborate ceremonies or complex activity — a power etiquette shares with ritual. Consider some such ceremony as the conferring of a degree, the instillation of officers, the reception of a Grand Lodge officer, a funeral ceremony, a public procession; the part each is to play is to a large extent prescribed in your Standard Work, Monitor, or in some other form of words or acts committed to memory. Over and above, there are a hundred and one required observances belonging to etiquette, which are necessary to the harmonious exemplification of the whole. These observances exist beforehand, each of a careful design that fits it exactly for its function. By means of these preexistent forms, learned by the participants, a large number of unrehearsed men are enabled to work smoothly in unison. Were there no other, this requirement would make etiquette a necessity in such a progressive society as ours.

In speaking of Masonic etiquette, it is necessary to emphasize the word "Masonic." Our etiquette is a unique creation, peculiar to the fraternity — absurd if used outside of its own setting but complete and beautiful within the Craft's framework. Some parts of our etiquette are optional, left to the good taste of the individual; other parts are prescribed by usage or by law, written or unwritten. Our etiquette belongs fundamentally to the organic body of Freemasonry and, as such, stands firmly on a level with the Landmarks, the Constitutions, the Ritual, and the Symbols. Why it is that, thus far, it has not received adequate treatment in our literature is difficult to understand. Perhaps our writers have labored under the impression that etiquette is a dry subject for which there would be no readers; if so, they are in error. Be that as it may, books on the subject have been few in number and not satisfactory in terms of material, which leads us to believe that such a complete manual would provide a service to the Craft across the borders of Jurisdictions.

Let us consider the exact status of a District Deputy Grand Master. He is the official and the personal representative of the Grand Master. It is, many times, impossible for a Grand Master to visit each lodge in the State, to have personal supervision of its workings, and to know each lodge intimately. Therefore, he appoints a Deputy, whose task is to visit each lodge in his District at least once yearly and then report annually to the Grand Master concerning the state of Freemasonry in the District. Your Book of Constitutions/Laws will define the duty of a District Deputy Grand Master more fully than space will permit here. But the point I wish to make is that on the occasion of an official visit to a lodge, the Deputy of the Grand Master out-ranks every other Grand Lodge officer except the Grand Master whom he represents.

But on occasions other than an official visit, or when the District Deputy Grand Master does not act for the Grand Master, the Deputy is out-ranked by every elected Grand Lodge officer.

Your Grand Lodge Monitor will provide clear instructions on how the District Deputy should be received in the lodge. It will also provide instructions on the reception of all other visitors, Grand Lodge or not. It would be wise to study the reception of visitors as they are simple rituals that take little time to master.

CHAPTER XVIII
THE BADGE OF A MASON

It's almost impossible to contemplate any phase of our ritualistic work and teaching and follow it through the Three Degrees without being profoundly impressed by how it builds up to a climax. Refer, for example, to the Scripture lessons. Nothing could be more impressive than, in the First Degree, the altogether lovely lesson on harmony in the 133rd Psalm, illustrated by the beautiful allegory of the dew of Hermon. In the Second Degree, we are given in allegory the life of a man built four square and true by the square of virtue, the plumb of upright character, and the plumb line of good judgment. Then there is the last Scripture lesson — powerful in its allegory, gentle in its teaching, and impressive in its strength: the lesson of feeble old age in its loneliness. To what climax do these studies lead up?

We might continue through the presentation of the Working Tools, the Obligations, Charges, Perambulations, and other parts of our work and point out how they help build up to a stirring pinnacle one by one.

For this study, however, let us turn our attention, especially to the lambskin or white leather apron, and study the various allusions to the badge of a Mason. For, after all, recognizing a climax is merely comparing the beginning and end of the subject under consideration.

The first allusion to the apron is subtle and occurs in the lodge's opening. The last time it appears in our ceremonies is at the grave of the deceased Brother — the beginning and the end, a whole life between!

The Master's first statement in opening the lodge is a compound sentence, the last half of which is an order dealing with the attire. Every Brother present must wear the clothing of a Mason, the Masonic apron!

The next allusion to the apron is made at its presentation to the candidate in the First Degree. It is then defined as an emblem of frequency and the badge of a Mason. The subtle use of the definite article "the" denotes that it is Mason's only badge. There is no other. Too few realize that the emblem one frequently sees on a ring, on the lapel of a coat, or on the bumper of a car is worn merely as a means of identification. The real badge of a Mason is his character. The apron is an emblem of that character. Let us, then, review the occasions when each is to be properly clothed with the apron.

At a lodge communication, all brethren, of course, wear the white apron. They are then at labor, and while at labor, they are "distinguished" by the badge of a Mason.

Give special attention to the word "distinguished," as used in our work by the Senior Warden. He never tells the candidate that brethren are "identified" or "organized" but that they are "distinguished" by the wearing of the apron. Here the word distinguished gives the idea of "honored." The man who, because of strength of character, may be distinguished by the right to wear the badge of a Mason is indeed honored. During a Grand Lodge communication, every brother present is to be clothed. This also applies to Grand Lodge ceremonies, such as the laying of cornerstones and the dedication of temples.

When a lodge conducts the funeral service for a deceased Brother, all Masons present, regardless of rank, are to be clothed with the white apron. Officers of the lodge and Grand

Lodge are to be clothed, as are the brethren, the symbolism teaching us that all men are equal in death. Very naturally, brethren are clothed according to their rank at Grand Lodge communications and Grand Lodge ceremonies.

The white apron symbolizes life's work so that when at last, the working tools are laid down, the apron is placed upon the casket. Between the presentation of the apron in the First Degree and the time the apron is laid upon the casket of the deceased brother, life has been lived, and that which symbolizes life is properly placed as the symbol of a life well spent as a Mason.

And so, my brethren, it is well to regard seriously the ornamentation of the apron. The badge of a Mason is not to be treated as a common thing. It symbolizes all that is high and fine in ideals; it distinguishes the man wearing it and teaches the lesson of humility.

A letter from the Rev. and R. ∴ W. ∴ Cuthbert C. Frost, then Grand Chaplain of the Grand Lodge of New York, may be appropriate here:

"In the New Testament, 1st Peter 5:5, the Apostle bids his friends, 'Gird yourselves with humility to serve one another.' The verb translated 'gird' is formed from a Greek noun meaning a servant's apron. The white scarf or apron was fastened to the girdle or vest to distinguish slaves from free men — when slaves were, of course, the only servants. It was, thus, not a mere utility garment, though, probably that was its origin but was worn actually as a badge of humble service. In his fine and illumining translation of the New Testament, Dr. Moffatt has phrased the above-quoted text with vivid and picturesque literalness:

'Indeed, you must all put on the Apron of humanity to serve one another.'

"Is not that exactly the significance of our Apron? A sign, not of pride, but the very negation of pride offering nothing that ministers to self-esteem, though too often so taken, rather proclaiming the deliberate refusal of all that separates self from the common welfare of all. When he accepts and wears it, the Mason is saying, in effect, what was said by One who illustrated his saying on a memorable occasion by taking a towel and girding Himself: 'I am in the midst of you and he that serveth.'

"I do not know how immediate or actual may be the historical connection between the service badge of ancient times and our Apron, but I feel that there is a kinship not so completely remote that it cannot give a pertinent and moving significance to our honored — and honoring — symbol. But whether or not the literal kinship can be established, the lambskin may be symbolized to the newest candidate, as well as to the oldest Past Master, that message of an olden time, so sorely needed in the heedless scramble of today, 'Indeed, you must all put on the Apron of humility to serve one another."

"*Candidus*" — a Latin word meaning "glittering white," symbolizing fair-mindedness without personal spite. This is precisely what is symbolized by the "badge of a Mason," the gleaming surface admonishing all who are so distinguished. At the ballot box, white ballots symbolize the absence of personal spite. White aprons — that someday a white stone may bear silent testimony that here was a man who wore the Badge of a Mason!

CHAPTER XIX
HAS YOUR LODGE A PLAN?

We have no work! Here is the most pitiful admission a Mason can make, particularly if he is the Worshipful Master of a lodge. And if it is the most pitiful admission a Master can make, it also seems one of the most frequent. Masters sometimes make the admission as an excuse for what they believe will be regarded as poor ritualistic work. Or they may give it as a reason for poor lodge attendance. And, of course, it is the old threadbare excuse for lack of interest on the part of the members.

When we attribute any of the ills of a lodge to the absence of work, we are entirely on the wrong track. Let's discuss, for a moment, the situation in which Masons would find themselves with no work for their lodges. Let's consider a community with its houses of worship filled at its services. It's a community in which harmony and brotherly love fill the hearts of all the citizens, and evil gossip, envy, and distrust are unheard of. It's a community in which poverty has no place, with jobs for all of its people and decent living wages paid to all, and in which children delight in learning and playing. A community with no civic problems and where a friendly hand clasp and a word of cheer are commonplace. A community, in short, in which life moves on with nothing to mar its serenity.

There is, of course, no community so happily situated that it affords no work for the Masons within its borders. As it seems, here is the trouble: through the years, we have built up, unthinkingly, of course, the idea that unless a lodge is busy conferring degrees, it has nothing to do. The question is repeatedly asked, "Are the lodges busy?" Meaning, of course, busy with degree work. And in asking the question, we seem wholly unable to comprehend that the conferring of degrees is not the whole business of a lodge. "Heresy," did I hear someone say? Well, if that be heresy, I challenge our unfortunate ways of thinking.

You see, many lodges during the Depression of the 1930s and before found themselves in a state of chronic discouragement because of the indifference of the members. For this condition, a lack of candidates was lightly blamed. And right here we were in serious error. I am thoroughly convinced that the real reason for the lack of interest in our lodges was a lack of discovering opportunities to minister to our personal human needs. There is the first obligation of the Craft. And it is a task we cannot afford to sidestep if our lodges are to function as they should.

Ritualistic work is necessary, of course. And it must be done accurately and with expression. Every lodge ought to find the quality of its degree work a source of satisfaction. And yet when we have no candidates to initiate, we should be eager in those things of human service that are essential to our legitimate work.

We must acquire that habit of seeking and finding work — and then doing it! The friendly smile and the encouraging words make our communities a better place to live. Here in such things is to be found the work of a Mason, work no less important than the performance of the ritual.

Yes, we have work! The advancing foot, even the barefoot, is emblematic of unselfishness, always ready for the errand of mercy!

Yes, we have work! The bended knee in the unselfish prayer — thought of the wants of others before our own!

Yes, we have work! Within the faithful breast, the hidden things, secrets vouchsafed us in hours of stress, all the never-to-be-divulged concerns of others, burdens of the anxious heart!

Yes, we have work! The pressure of a sustaining hand for support in times of stress!

Yes, we have work! The kind words, the comforting thoughts, the needed advice, the kindly admonition to warn of approaching danger!

And then there is the deeper work of our internal foundation. If we are to help our fellow human beings by our example, how do we know that our example is of any value? The willingness to be of service is not always enough. One may have a sincere and heartfelt desire to help another with a legal problem, but if he has no legal training, his assistance may result in only additional problems for the one he wishes to help. If one untrained in medicine attempts to render advanced medical treatment on someone, then obvious problems could arise. The same is true for one untrained in plumbing, real estate, or any service that requires specialized training. In the true sense of the word, a Freemason has received specialized training. But have we all been properly and sufficiently trained? Do we correctly understand the meanings of our teachings?

Do we have no work? Our work is never-ending. If we have no degree scheduled, we have the work of teaching our lessons. The symbolism of the rituals can and should be examined and explored. A doctor who knows nothing of medicine is of little value to a hospital. So, of what value is a Freemason who knows nothing of Masonry to his lodge or the world? And who is at fault if a Mason knows nothing of

Masonry? Is it true that you have no work? Our work is never-ending.

Here is the Mason's Trestleboard, the true business of a Masonic lodge. Let it *never* be said, "We have no work!"

CHAPTER XX
MASONRY MILITANT

Many years ago, a little boy (me) trudged along with the aid of an old gentleman. The road was long, and the day hot. The boy looked up at his grandfather with awe from time to time, wondering what secrets lay back in the thoughtful face. Only that morning, the youngster had heard his grandfather say something about Masonry, respectfully, as one speaks of sacred things. What had been said didn't matter — the tone of his grandfather's voice awakened the boy's curiosity.

This "Masonry" business persisted in his mind. What was it all about? Maybe Grandfather would know — didn't he know everything? So, one day —

"Grandpa, are you a Mason?"
"I am," replied the old gentleman.
"Can I be a Mason?"
"When you are of legal age, you can try," was the reply.
"What is a Mason, Grandfather?"

I have forgotten his reply. But I decided then and there that I would "try."

Years passed, and in the fullness of time, there came a day when I went to a cedar chest and took out a white lambskin apron, somewhat yellowed with age. I smoothed out the wrinkles and laid them on the casket of the man I revered, not only as my grandfather but as an upright man and Mason whose life had tremendously influenced mine. I never saw him wear a Masonic pin or badge — his Masonry was worn in his heart. He lived his Masonry daily, and few, save the brethren of his lodge, knew him to be a Mason.

The respect for our institution, which I received from my grandfather, was intensified by the circumstance of my initiation. I shall never forget the quiet, respectful atmosphere of the preparation room when the Master of Ceremony prepared the young candidate. The Worshipful Master, a commanding figure of a man, seemed to tower as he stood in the East. The story of that night might have been ruined if I had been ill-treated, but it wasn't, and I felt then a convection that has never left me. I felt as if I was taking part in something of profound importance.

The Master of Ceremony is the first to receive a candidate. He must maintain an atmosphere of quiet dignity and respect. Like other officers, the emblem on their apron tells the story of their responsibility. Not only is the apron a badge of a Mason, but it becomes, by the emblem, the badge of the particular function of the officer. The emblem of the Master of Ceremony is two crossed swords, as against the Tyler's — one sword placed vertically in the center. The appropriateness of the sword lies in the fact that it is the implement of one who guards.

I believe the great body of dormant Masons would be greatly lessened if more attention were paid to properly preparing their minds in the preparation room. And by "dormant Masons," I allude to those who indicate no interest in Masonry except by paying their dues.

What is most to be desired is a body of Masons so militant in their Masonry that finally, through an activated Craft, Masonry becomes triumphant Masonry militant! This would be a Craft keenly aware of the service opportunities, making the world a little happier and brighter, bringing a smile to weary lips, and easing burdened shoulders. For all this, we may lay the foundation in the preparation room.

The crossed swords signify the care to be used in preserving the correct atmosphere of the preparation room. And since the swords appear as the emblem, perhaps we may infer that they are emblematic of the care to be exercised in a double preparation of the mind and body.

As is often worth repeating, everything in our work has a reason. And now that we know "why" this particular badge of a Mason is used for the proxy of the Senior Deacon let us regard his work in his contact with candidates as worthy of the respect of all.

It would be well if Masons regarded the preparation room with the same respect they hold for the space between the altar and the East.

CHAPTER XXI
THE "IN-BETWEEN"

Here is a question that should be asked by every Mason who has not already asked and answered it for himself: "I want an education in Masonry. What books should I buy first?" Certainly, should every initiate and newly made Mason ask the question. It is good to see those Masters who, to assimilate their newly made brethren into the lodge, want to impart something of the traditions, history, symbolism, and allegory of the Craft.

All this is to the good, but in this chapter, I'd like to stress the fact that, while the importance of Masonically educating the newly made Masons and our junior officers cannot be over-stated, we do seem to give too little thought to the "in-between." This man in the lodge was raised "some time ago" and is not considered a newly raised Mason or a lodge officer. We do too little to impress upon him that the task of real Masonry is more than the mere passing and raising of candidates.

Why is it, then, that practically all of our efforts in Masonic education are directed to the top and the bottom of the membership of a lodge? Why does organized effort seem to be directed principally toward the Worshipful Master and his officers on the one hand and the other to the newly raised?

An answer to the question is, for the new Mason, that we are anxious to actualize the business of becoming a Craftsman to the highest degree possible. We seem to set up in the mind of the officer working through the chairs a conviction that what the lodge amounts to in the future will be pretty much "up to him." His impression is that over time, as he assumes the East and becomes the directing head (and likewise, we hope, the directing force) of the lodge, his members will look to him for leadership. So, we want him educated.

And that is one of the places where the "In-Between" comes in. Who, if not he, will inspire the "newly made" and officers to be trained in Masonry, each in his job? Who, if not he, will be the pool from which flows the improvement of the new Craftsman, regardless of his place in the line? Remember that we are all Master Masons, and that the implication is that every one of us is skilled in all the techniques of the Art. But are we? And, if we are not, how do we help properly educate *all* members?

Thus, it comes about that each Mason must ask himself, "What am I doing to build the Stewards into efficient Masters of Ceremony, men who will have a proper conception of their duty, who will know that they must preserve the proper atmosphere in the preparation room. And likewise, as these men, in turn, become Deacons, and the Deacons become Wardens — what am I doing to develop a deep sense of responsibility in them, year by year, in their various offices."

And by the same token, each "In-Between" must ask himself about the newly-raised man. All the food that a man can eat, no matter how hungry he may be, will do him no good unless he can assimilate the life-giving property of that food. This is true in a lodge — all of our members will be of little practical value to the organization unless each, side-liners and all, shows an active interest in these new men as Brother Masons, seeking to build them into something more than a mere dues-paying name on the roster. We have too little conception of the latent possibilities in those around us. A bit of encouragement, and a helping hand, will give all members a tremendous boost and aid them to be assets to the lodge instead of liabilities.

Freemasonry is always in need of one thing above all else — leadership, embodied in the Worshipful Masters of lodges; leadership expressed in terms of vision, imagination, vitality, and all those other qualities of mind and heart that make a man a leader and not just a follower. For this reason, the man who approaches the East owes it to himself and his lodge and community to develop himself so that he may fulfill all the implications of his title, "Master!"

More and more Wardens are asking for information on matters pertaining to the Mastership. Perhaps this is due to special activities carried on by Grand Masters in recent years, such as Area and District Meetings, and in the services and facilities offered by the Grand lodges, which have enjoyed a wider acceptance among lodge officers with each succeeding year.

In past years, there seemed to be less interest, except on the part of a comparative few, in this matter of preparation for the East. Today, one sees a profound and welcome change. Workable efforts have also been put forth to increase the usefulness of new members. "Usefulness" may be a strange word, but he must learn before a man can be helpful. Educational booklets, reading lists, branch libraries, study clubs, videos, and lending of books — these services in many lodges are recommended to the newly-raised brethren as well as the "In-Betweens."

Thus, we see that officers, particularly administrative officers, benefit from our education efforts. While at the same time, more (a great deal more) is being done for the new initiates than ever. When we contemplate this situation, we must concede that in between these two Masonic groups is a practically untouched educational field. The great body of "In-Between" Masons need more than what they receive. They benefit from Masonic education and a mastery of every aspect of the Craft — its history, philosophy, and symbolism. The details of its organizational machinery become the inspiration and source of Masonic wisdom. And, in the end, it will be a measure of the training given to our newly made Masons and officers.

One of our difficulties has been that we are too inclined to consider what will help us now rather than what will affect the Craft in time. A plan that cares only for the present and does not consider the future is useless. We need vision. We must look ahead. Furthermore, as far as this "In-Between" problem is concerned, I believe that the man who submits himself to formal training, which assembles with his brethren with that object in view, will find his interests re-awakened. His lodge should also discover that he is an asset, not a liability. The eighty percent of our dues-paying members will, in part at least, be not a variable entity but a dependable part of our lodges.

From practical experience and observation over a considerable period of years, I know that it is practicable to introduce a System of Masonic education into our lodges, and the results will not disappoint us.

CHAPTER XXII
COMMITTEES

THE INVESTIGATION COMMITTEE

The first committee I would like to discuss is one we have all experienced before joining Masonry. This would be the process from the investigation committee to the ballot box.

I believe that the actions of an investigation committee and those who ballot on a candidate may well be the most profound and sobering actions we take in Masonry. When we stop and think about this, we are passing judgment on the worthiness of another human being. How can we be qualified to do such a thing? And yet it is something we must do.

Any thinking person will realize what a tremendous responsibility is placed upon us. I can think of no way to disrespect Masonry greater than an investigation committee that is lax or negligent in its duties.

The sad truth is that I have seen far too many investigation committees that do little more than learn the candidate's name and address. The investigation of a candidate, if we can call it that, is far more often than not left to a third-party paid investigation service. These investigation companies provide the basic information about a candidate and then inform the lodge if the candidate shows up in their records as being arrested for a crime. Time after time, in many areas, such paid investigation companies are shown to provide incorrect or incomplete information. Lodges pay for these services and accept the information received as fact, whether it is or not. And yet, far too many lodges use such companies as their sole manner of investigating a candidate.

Grand Lodges apparently know that if they did not require this basic investigation, then there is a good chance that no investigation would occur in too many lodges. How sad.

An investigation committee should be composed of at least three members of the lodge, one of them being a knowledgeable Past Master. They should understand their significance and responsibility to the lodge and the whole of Freemasonry.

If paid investigation services are used, they should be the investigation's start, not the end. The investigation committee should have no preconceived opinion of the candidate. They should simply investigate him with an open mind to see if he is worthy of being considered a member of their own family — a brother.

The members of an investigation committee must know the laws of Masonry. They should be dedicated, sincere, have no biases, and be totally committed to fairly investigating the candidate in a manner respectful to both the lodge and the candidate.

If the lodge does not have qualified members capable of serving conscientiously on an investigation committee, then frankly, why does the lodge exist? The choices are to do the job correctly, learn how to do it correctly, or close shop. This responsibility is too great to be entrusted to those with limited Masonic knowledge or those with less than noble intentions.

And now, we come to the ballot box. There is no greater test of the integrity of a Mason and no greater trust in that integrity than with the ballot box. I don't believe any instruction on using the ballot box is necessary here, as it has been explained to all Masons in their lodge. But I will point out that because the balloting is done in secret, at least in all jurisdictions of which I am familiar, a special trust is displayed. The lodge places full trust in the integrity of all Masons that they will ballot in the best interest of Freemasonry and with the honor expected of Freemasons.

Because the ballot is secret, that trust is backed up by the inability to expose anyone who may violate the integrity of the ballot box. Anyone who would use the ballot box in an unMasonic manner is protected by the secrecy of the ballot. They will only answer in the next world for their actions.

Because lodges of Freemasons have Masonic trials, it is obvious that not all who join completely understand or wish to follow the teachings of Freemasonry. Simply put, we do have bad apples among us. At times, jealousy, revenge, bigotry, or any of many less-than-noble reasons influence someone to misuse the ballot box to the detriment of all.

If someone knows of a valid reason someone should not be allowed to join us, then this information should be shared with the Master where the candidate has petitioned or the investigation committee.

We have a responsibility to Freemasonry to see that none join us who are morally unfit or for any other valid reason would be viewed as unsuitable for Freemasonry. This is a responsibility that we owe to Freemasonry, the lodge, and all Masons who have gone before us. It is a serious matter that we must not let slide out of uncertainty.

If anyone has questions about whether someone is suitable for membership, or if there are questions about the fitness of someone joining Masonry, they should contact their Worshipful Master or knowledgeable Masons for advice.

But while joining Freemasonry is not a right of anyone, it should not be denied to anyone who desires to join, and is worthy, without good cause. Personal disagreements, rumors, jealousy, bigotry, business considerations, or countless petty reasons must not guide anyone to deny a good man joining Masonry.

Sadly, because this has happened more than a few times, some jurisdictions have changed the balloting procedure, with some requiring more than one black cube to reject. Abuses do happen. When they do happen, they can forever change attitudes for some.

THE EDUCATION COMMITTEE

Consider the phrase, "Things we learned in school." A child can learn in many different places and by many different means. A child learns from his family, from reading, watching television, interacting with others, and from countless sources. The phrase, however, focuses on learning in a classroom setting. Regardless of that qualification, the phrase is still general enough that we have no idea if the learning is the alphabet taught in kindergarten or advanced calculus taught in a university. The same is true of Masonic education. When we speak of "Masonic education," it could apply to a new Mason studying for the first time with his instructor or a Mason of many years studying the finer points of Masonic symbolism. The term "Masonic education" spans all aspects of Masonic learning. So should the lodge's committee on Masonic education.

A lodge's Education Committee should be composed of members with such knowledge in Masonry that they can be of service in all areas of Masonic education. The fact is that there are but few activities of the lodge where Masonic education does not play a role. It is also a fact that far too many lodges do not make use, or proper use, of this important committee.

It is difficult to pinpoint exactly where one's education in Masonry begins as so many non-Masons receive their first Masonic education by observing Masons' actions in non-Masonic settings. All Masons teach Masonry through their actions outside of the lodge. Masons who learn nothing in the lodge pass on what they have learned (or not learned) and can sometimes very poorly represent Masonry in the profane world. An active education committee, along with a creative and dedicated Worshipful Master, can provide comprehensive and well-balanced educational programs at every meeting and special classes for degree work or other activities. With careful planning and organization, an education plan can provide excellent service to all lodge members.

When a petition is received by the lodge, the Investigation Committee should begin its work by following a plan created by the Education Committee. A step-by-step road map for the Investigation Committee can provide invaluable assistance to this most important committee and give greater assurance that their work will be properly done. The road map, however, should be general. No two investigations are alike, and it is impossible to preplan for every situation an investigation committee can encounter. I am aware of one lodge which put on a very successful series of plays in the lodge showing various examples of proper and improper investigation techniques. It is an excellent example of proper Masonic education. The time between a successful ballot and the EA degree is also important for the Education Committee.

Freemasonry is a descendant of the Ancient Mystery Schools. Non-Masons do not join Masonry but are *initiated* into it. It is an important distinction, and steps must be taken for a valid initiation. One step is for the candidate to be in the proper frame of mind for the initiation. The investigation or education committee (or a combination) should meet with the candidate soon before his initiation. General information about the history and philosophy of Masonry should be given to the candidate. Some of the curious words and phrases (such as "Worshipful Master") should be explained to the candidate. It should be explained that Masonry is not a college fraternity, and humiliation, ridicule, or trifling with the candidate are prohibited. All the information which can be given to the candidate should be given, and all efforts should be made to impress upon him the seriousness of what he is about to undertake.

The period following the EA initiation is another critical time for the Education Committee. The initiation might have been as impressive and well-received as could be hoped, but the work is far, far from complete. I well remember a young man who was eager to join Masonry. He petitioned a lodge and anxiously awaited when he would receive his EA degree. The Investigation Committee told the young man that the lodge did not believe in or participate in the "one-day classes" where a candidate would receive all the degrees at once. They said it provides the candidates with no opportunity to absorb what they received before receiving another degree. This pleased the young man. He wanted to experience all that Masonry offered. They told him that he would need to learn and pass an exam in open lodge before he could advance to the next degree. The young man said that he was ready to do what was needed.

The night of the initiation came, and the young man was deeply moved and impressed. The Worshipful Master told him at the end of the evening that someone would contact him and tell him how he could start his instructions. A month passed, and no one from the lodge contacted the new EA. Confused, the young man phoned one of the members of the Investigation Committee. Sounding a bit irritated, the committee member told the young brother he misunderstood. He said that EAs need to contact their instructors to see about starting the instructions. The young brother said he had never been told who his instructor was or how to contact him. The committee member said that he would need to phone the Worshipful Master but said that he did not have his phone number handy. He said he would call the young man back in a day or two. The following week he called with the phone number and said that the brother would need to call to set up his instructions. The EA phoned the Worshipful Master, who again told him that he would be contacted and said that he was not yet contacted because the brother who did the instruction was on vacation. Another month passed before the EA was phoned and told that his instructions could begin. By now, the EA was feeling a bit left out and frustrated. The experience was no longer fresh in his mind. A meeting was scheduled for the following week. The instructor told the EA that he could spare half an hour for the instructions yet spent half of that time showing him his house and, in general, chit-chat. Not much actual work was done, and when the instructor said that his time was up, the EA asked when the next session could start. The instructor said it was up to the EA and that he should phone him the following week. The EA phoned three times before he was able to reach the instructor. The instructor said that he was under the weather and said that he should phone him the following week.

Six months after his initiation, the EA received a total of three instruction sessions. Feeling hurt, ignored, and very frustrated, he gave up. He stopped calling and trying to set up his instructions and, guess what? Not a single member of the lodge phoned him to find out what was wrong. He never again set foot in that lodge. Is anyone surprised?

This lodge failed in just about every way imaginable. There is no excuse for their disservice to this brother.

When a lodge accepts a candidate for the degrees in Masonry, they take upon themselves a serious responsibility. On the night of the EA initiation, the Worshipful Master should introduce the new brother to the members of the Education Committee and his instructor. Phone numbers from everyone should be exchanged. The instructor should present the new EA with several choices of days to meet to begin instructions and ask which day would suit him best. Instructions should begin as soon as possible, certainly within a week. The EA should not be told something like, "Give us a call, and we can set up instructions." The EA may not call, and many reasons could have nothing to do with a lack of interest. The burden should not be on the EA to set up instructions. Dates for instructions should be given to the EA, and his burden should be on keeping the appointments set by the instructor and doing the work required. The Worshipful Master and the Education Committee members should phone the new EA every week or so to see how his instructions are going (even though they might be getting full reports from the instructor). Contact must be made and kept up with the EA. If any EA degrees are taking place in their lodge or nearby lodges, the EA should be invited to them. He must be made to feel welcome, a part of the lodge, and that his progress is being watched with great interest. To ignore a new EA is disgraceful.

The Education Committee's work does not end with candidate instruction. The committee should be available for any lodge member, especially officers. Officers who cannot perform the opening and closing rituals promote disinterest in the lodge. I remember one Junior Warden who needed prompting with nearly every second word of his ritual. I spoke with him after the meeting, and he told me that he did not have time to learn the ritual but that the lodge should be happy to have someone in the chair. What a sad situation! This brother became the Worshipful Master of the lodge two years later, and two years after that, the lodge ceased to exist. Was this brother or the whole lodge to blame?

Those who advance through the chairs should make the time to properly learn the Work. If they do not have the time to learn the Work, they should not make themselves available for the chairs, be removed from office (if appointed), or not be elected to the next chair. The members of the Education Committee should work with those seeking the chairs and advise the Worshipful Master of their knowledge of the Work before they are appointed to any chair. By the time they are elected to the Junior Warden's station, they should have proven themselves competent in all of the Work of the lodge, including that of the East.

Some years back, I worked in a very stressful job. One day I had what I thought was a heart attack. It turned out to be stress. I asked the doctor if stress could cause an actual heart attack. He told me that as far as the heart was concerned, stress was like tapping on a piece of glass with a hammer. He could not say if or when the glass would break, but he could certainly say that it was not a good thing to do. The same is true of Masonic education. No one can say if a lodge composed of officers with little knowledge of their work will cease to exist in a few years or ever. All that can be said is that it is a sickly lodge where the work is not properly done. All lodges need a good diet and exercise program of Masonic education.

The Education Committee should participate in all areas of Masonic education, from new EAs to experienced members and officer education. A successful lodge will have a proactive Education Committee, which will create educational programs for the lodge and find ways to educate the entire membership through workshops or individual instructions.

THE FINANCE COMMITTEE

A certain lodge was well served by a Treasurer for over 20 years. At an educational workshop, a new Worshipful Master learned of the role of the Finance Committee. All that was said made sense, but he realized that his lodge did not have such a committee, and he did not remember such a committee ever existing in the lodge. He set about correcting that error and appointed the committee. He gave them the instructions that he had learned at the workshop.

When he learned of the formation of the new finance committee, the Treasurer turned in his resignation. He said that he had never been so insulted and that if the Worshipful Master distrusted or questioned his work, he no longer wished to serve. What an unnecessary shame! What a misunderstanding!

The role of the Finance Committee is not to question the performance or honesty of anyone. It is simply a system of responsible checks and balances. Anyone can make an error, and it is wise to have more than one set of eyes look at what is so important to the successful running of the lodge.

Most lodges have the Finance Committee's existence stipulated in the lodge bylaws, and some may and may not serve on the committee (most elected officers are not eligible). However, we still find more lodges than might be expected who have never heard of this committee.

The Finance Committee should examine all financial records of the lodge and report its findings to the lodge at predetermined meetings. Some lodges have the committee report once a year, but others report quarterly. The Finance Committee can also assist with the financial planning of the lodge, such as determining which investments might prove most useful for the lodge. Such a committee can be of service and aid to any Treasurer.

In all cases, the Finance Committee should have a productive and brotherly relationship with all officers.

THE ENTERTAINMENT COMMITTEE

"All work and no play makes Jack a dull boy." It's true. If we properly understand the teachings of Masonry, we understand that one of the great lessons is for us to reach balance in our lives. Productive work is important to a Mason, but so is productive refreshment. Silliness has no place in a lodge's degrees, but a creative Entertainment Committee can provide a valuable service. The Entertainment Committee should work hand in hand with the Junior Warden, Treasurer and Finance Committee so that no problems might arise with over-budgeting dinners or other forms of refreshment. The committee must know exactly what money they have available to plan their events. In truth, many good events can be had with little or no lodge money. Taking their cue from the Junior Warden, this committee can provide suggestions for light entertainment, such as music for a portion of a presentation, a speaker, or light refreshments following a meeting. The committee can also plan a special occasion evening, such as a planned banquet. It is truly an open book as to how this committee can operate.

Below are just a few program suggestions that have worked successfully for lodges. This list certainly should not be considered the extent of what could be suggested by an entertainment committee. A creative committee can develop very fitting, enjoyable, and unique programs. One more point should be stated: I know of several very active lodges which never confer degrees on stated meetings. They always call special meetings for degree work. The logic behind their calling these special meetings is sound. In the fall, when the Senior Warden plans the programs for the upcoming year, he has no way of knowing if the lodge will have degree work in September (or any month) of the following year. This is especially true if the lodge has a history of putting on but a few degrees each year. Each and every lodge meeting is an opportunity to build interest and strength. Stated meetings are reserved for stated business — meaning the planned programs of the lodge. Degree work is considered a special event, and it is justified to call a special meeting for this type of special event. It only adds interest and importance to the event.

Ideas for lodge programs (in the lodge or outside the lodge):

Scholarship Awards Night — The lodge can select an outstanding high school or middle school student and present them with an award plaque. It is a great public event for the lodge, and dinner can follow. Some lodges select one male and one female student, but the details are very flexible and can be decided by the lodge.

Masonic Debate Night — Select a Masonic subject where sides can be taken (one-day classes, 18-year-old membership, ritual memorization, etc.) and select two lodge members to debate the subject. With a little effort, this can be a most interesting program. Obvious care should be taken in the subject selection. Any highly controversial or "sore" subject that could enflame passions should be avoided.

Youth Night — Invite the local DeMolay or Rainbow Chapter to your lodge to "show their stuff." Light or elaborate refreshments can follow.

Theater Night — Plan a theater party for family and friends and escort the widows. It can be at a movie or stage play. One lodge plans such events at a local "Oldies but Goodies" theater that shows old black and white and silent films. Great fun!

Grand Lodge Night — Invite a Grand Lodge officer to attend one of your meetings and have him speak on a subject familiar to him.

Historical Site Visitation — Visit a local historical site. If the site has Masonic connections, then plan for the Master of Ceremonies (or any selected officer) to give a talking tour. With a bit of pre-planning, this can be a most impressive program.

Research Lodge Speakers — Masonic history, clandestine lodges, women in Masonry, the development of Masonry (or the Masonic ritual) in your state, country, or the world. You might be amazed at the great and informative subjects a knowledgeable Masonic historian can provide for your lodge.

Monthly Dinner/Lunch Club — lodge members, wives, and friends can meet for a "pay your way" dinner or lunch at the restaurant of their choice. It's a great way for non-Masons to get to know Masons, wives to get to know each other, and all to have a great time.

Volunteer Work Parties for lodge Visibility — Select a modest home needing clean-up and paint (perhaps a Masonic widow's home); clean up a local park, etc.

Picnic or Barbecue — Encourage your members to bring their friends and neighbors.

Sports Event — A number of lodges have successful gatherings revolving around any popular sport with the members, be it golf, bowling, fishing, or anything.

Speakers — Masonic speakers can be an important part of lodge meetings and banquets. Be sure to read and reread Chapter II, "Courtesies of the East," for important tips on how speakers should be treated. One caution! It's not wise to have speakers at every meeting or too often. It is also wise to talk to others who have heard a speaker before you commit to a program with him. The brethren can get bored with long pointless speeches. An interesting speaker can create great interest. A long-winded, mono-tone speaker with no clear message can be almost painful.

Family Night Program — Make sure that your members know to invite their non-Masonic friends and neighbors. Give them ample notice. Many jurisdictions publish pamphlets for non-Masons who might wish to learn more about Masonry. This would be the perfect time to stock up on and pass out these pamphlets.

Potluck Dinners — Before your Family Night programs, invite your friends and neighbors. Note: theme dinners make the evening seem less ordinary.

Mason of the Year Award — Select a member of the lodge (or any lodge) who has contributed greatly to your lodge or Masonry as a whole and present him with an award. Honorary Lodge Membership (non-dues paying) is a wonderful acknowledgment for a brother from another lodge. Take advantage of this night to also invite your non-Masonic friends and neighbors.

Past Masters' Night — This should be one of the set programs every year. This is the night when you recognize the Past Masters of your lodge and the contributions they have made to the Craft.

Secretary's Night — This should be another set program. The Lodge Secretary is a tireless worker, and it is most fitting that he be acknowledged.

Table lodge — In those jurisdictions where it is permitted, the Table lodge can be a valuable and enjoyable way of promoting Masonic knowledge and good fellowship. Some Grand Lodges have their rituals for use at Table lodges and strict guidelines for the conduct of Table lodges.

Patriotic Program — (Washington's Birthday; Memorial Day; Flag Day; Fourth of July; Veteran's Day; Etc.) Patriotic programs are always popular. You can get a lot of people involved, especially the Youth Groups. You can usually get some good publicity for well-planned patriotic activities. "Love of Country" is a basic emotion that needs "recharging" frequently.

THE CONTACT COMMITTEE

The name should say it all. The Contact Committee should be charged with staying in touch with the membership, and that would include widows. One of the worst situations that can develop in a lodge is the "them and us" attitude. That would be a situation where the regularly attending members and those who seldom visit the lodge view each other as different groups. They become divided and split rather than being one and the same. It is a dangerous situation. It is, sadly, the same situation that can develop between lodges and their Grand Lodge.

Sometimes life can be filled with events that prevent a member from attending the lodge. After a while, he begins to feel less and less a part of the lodge. He may care, but the lodge becomes "them," and attending meetings might become difficult — even if things settle down and he is perfectly able to attend. He might begin to feel awkward and find that staying home is just less complicated. The lodge might view non-attending members as lacking in loyalty or dedication. The "them and us" gap widens and sometimes becomes impossible to bridge. Both the lodge and the member lose out. Another problem with losing contact with members is that each year, many lodges drop members or suspend them NPD because they have no idea where they are located. The members moved and simply forgot to send the lodge a new address. Out of sight, out of mind.

The Contact Committee should contact each lodge member no less than every six months. If a lodge is just starting a contact committee, then the committee members should realize that some of the members being contacted might not have heard from anyone in the lodge for many years. The member being called may be wholly unknown to

116

any of the officers. In truth, calling such a member should be more of an introduction than anything else. If you call a member who has not been to the lodge in many years, it is not wise to immediately push the "Come visit us at the lodge" speech. Tell the members you are on the contact committee and wish to know how they are doing. If a brother seems receptive, ask if you can call again. Give the brother another call in a week or so to see how he is doing. If he seems appreciative of the call, tell him of the date of the next lodge meeting and ask if he would like a ride to the lodge. If he does not seem inclined to go, do not push him. Give him an open invitation to both the lodge and a ride to the lodge. If you learn of any health problems, ask the brother if he would be receptive to a personal visit. The news of the brother's condition and a visit report should be given to the lodge. Unless a brother tells you not to call him again, call regularly. He is your brother.

THE NEWSLETTER COMMITTEE

Most lodges have some sort of newsletter sent out to the membership. Often, the writer/editor/publisher/and mailer of the newsletter is either the Secretary or Worshipful Master. While no one can doubt the brothers' good intentions or hard work, a one-man show rarely provides all that could be given if more hands help. A newsletter is an extremely effective tool for any lodge. Lodges should make the most of this tool with a committee to handle all aspects of the publication (writing, editing, production, mailing, etc.).

It is rare today to find a lodge where no one owns or has access to a computer. Computer programs can prove a tremendous asset to anyone who wishes to publish a newsletter, as almost all of them have a newsletter template where all that is necessary is to fill in the blanks with your content. Once the newsletter is completed, printing a copy and taking it to your local printer (or printing it yourself) is simple. It is also a simple task in the computer age to create a PDF file of your newsletter and e-mail it to the members with e-mail addresses. This saves the lodge postage and gets the members their newsletter much faster.

A good lodge newsletter should contain useful content that is well laid out and easy to find. There are certain things that no newsletter should be without:

Table of Contents — A table of contents is good practice because it lets readers know what's inside the issue and allows them to skip right to the articles they want to read.

Message from the Worshipful Master — A must in every lodge newsletter is an article written by the Worshipful Master. This is a chance for the Master to promote upcoming events and activities, present a bit of Masonic education, or express personal feelings or opinions.

Upcoming Events — Upcoming events should be a big part of the newsletter. A well-formatted calendar of events should be included with every issue and should be in the same place for each issue. By keeping the calendar in the same spot, readers can find it quickly when they want it.

Past Events — What would a newsletter be without articles about recent events that provide details for those not present? These types of articles get the word out about special events and can include promotions for similar upcoming events.

Reminders — Reminders of events and meetings are another great method of promotion. Reminders should stand out and be easily seen.

Pictures — Photos add spice to any newsletter. A whole page of only text can turn off a reader or overwhelm him. Adding pictures to your newsletter will help you hold the reader's attention longer. However, when using pictures in a newsletter, you must ensure they will print clearly. A photo that is too blurry or dark to be recognized is worse than no photo at all.

Contact Information — Include information about how to contact the officers. This is one of the largest forms of communication within the lodge, and if a member has a question, he should have the contact information for the right people available in the newsletter. If the lodge has a website, you should also provide the web address in this section.

Organizing the information into a lodge newsletter can be daunting if you have little or no journalism experience. Here are a few tips that might help you provide your information or message in the best way possible.

The basic rule of thumb for organizing content is that the most important information should come at the beginning of the newsletter. The front page is the place for all the big stories everyone should read. Unless something very important has happened which should be known or is of interest to all, upcoming events should be the lead in your newsletter. Following that should be articles about past events. In most cases, more people will be interested in what will happen than in what has already passed.

Develop a Uniform Style — From issue to issue, the basic style of the newsletter should remain the same. Text, boxes, and headers/footers should all stay the same from issue to issue. By doing this, your newsletter will have a much smoother and familiar feel.

Keep Layout the Same within Each Issue — Keeping the same layout within each issue is very important. Keeping the design the same from page to page gives the newsletter a cleaner feel and makes for a better publication overall. Pick one font style and stay with it.

Keep Content Layout from Issue to Issue — In addition to having the same style from issue to issue, some articles should remain in the same place. For example, the Worshipful Master's message, calendar, web address, contact information, and table of contents should all remain in the same place. These are items that readers look for, and by knowing exactly where they are, they can save a lot of trouble.

Report Don't Editorialize — The Worshipful Master's Message section allows him to write his thoughts or opinions on anything. You can have an editorial section where selected individuals or anyone also publishes thoughts and opinions. No other articles should contain opinions. When reporting on an upcoming or past event, refrain from giving any opinion on the subject — pro or con. Upcoming or past events should be reported, including all details, but no comments on the writer's thoughts about the event. Editorializing news articles gives a most unprofessional feel to a newsletter.

LODGE WEBSITE COMMITTEE

It was not too many years ago when no need for such a committee existed. Today just about every Grand Lodge has a website, as do countless lodges. For the wise lodge, a website can be something of an extension and elaboration of their newsletter. It should provide basic contact information as well as news and lodge information.

As far back as the 1800s, quite a few lodges used their local newspapers as their "bulletin board." Notices would be published for degrees, election of officers, and other events. Even when nothing special was happening, you could find notices with just the lodge name, address, and either the Worshipful Master or Secretary in the newspapers. In the electronic age, this function is served by the lodge website.

Before a lodge should consider a website, they should check with their Grand Lodge. Some jurisdictions have rules for lodge websites, and you should check these out before creating your website. The second important point is that if your lodge has no members with website building or managing experience, don't attempt to build one without getting expert help.

Lodge websites can be simple pages with little more than contact information or elaborate sites with many pages, features, and other "fancy stuff." Regardless of how complex or simple a website is, it must be updated regularly (translate: weekly or monthly). It presents a very poor message when someone visits a lodge website to be greeted by the smiling faces of officers from three years ago. Remember also that yours is a MASONIC website. Sports news, stocks, and many other interesting "add-ons" that can be found for websites are inappropriate for a Masonic site. Keep what you offer on the site related to Freemasonry.

Just like the lodge newsletter, a website can be a wonderful informational tool. Everything published in a newsletter can be posted on the website, and still, much more is available. Some lodge websites have photo albums of special events, officers, and historical images from the past. Guest books are available so visitors can leave comments (an ideal way to stay in touch). Links can take visitors to sites deemed important to the lodges — often Grand Lodge or sister lodge sites. Below are just a few suggested Masonic sites that provide a world of useful Masonic information and services. Linking to these sites (as well as making use of them) provides a service to all Masons.

The Masonic Service Association of North America —
(www.msana.com) — MSANA was formed in 1919 to provide services to its member Grand lodges that they would find difficult to provide for themselves. The MSA publishes the valuable "Short Talk Bulletins" and provides countless services to Grand lodges, lodges, and individual Masons. The website has useful, interesting, and necessary Masonic information and services.

George Washington National Memorial —
(www.gwmemorial.org) — Dedicated to the memory of George Washington-Patriot, President, and Mason, as an expression of the Masonic fraternity's faith in the principles of civil and religious liberty and orderly government. This website has a wealth of Masonic information.

Wikipedia Category: Freemasonry —
(http://en.wikipedia.org/wiki/Freemasonry) — This free online encyclopedia has an excellent collection of information on the Craft and in-depth explanations of its social relevance.

Anti-Masonry: Points of View —
(www.masonicinfo.com) — Yes, anti-Masons exist. While most Masons simply dismiss the often-nonsensical claims made by the anti-Masons, some anti-Masons possess enough skill to make their charges sound plausible. Bro. Ed King created this "anti-Masonic exposure" site with the goal of exposing the tactics, charges, and claims made by the anti-Masons. This is a very detailed and extensive site covering

many issues and personalities. It is certainly worth a visit if you encounter an anti-Mason sounding like he knows what he is talking about.

Hosting your lodge website is the dollars and cents aspect of having this tool. If your lodge is on a budget (most are), you might wish to try one of the free website hosting services. A quick internet search can provide you with several such services and the tools they use to build your site. For a most reasonable fee, (sometimes free) you can find good hosting providers. In addition, some Grand lodges, or other Masonic bodies, provide free web space for lodges. It only requires knowing what you want and putting forth a small amount of effort to find it.

In all, a lodge website, properly maintained, can be both enjoyable, an expression of the lodge's personality, and a helpful information tool.

APPENDIX A

THE POWER OF THE WORSHIPFUL MASTER
THE SHORT TALK BULLETIN
The Masonic Service Association of the United States
Volume 7 Number 8
August 1929
Author Unknown

The incumbent of the Oriental Chair has powers peculiar to his station; powers far greater than those of the President of a society or the Chairman of a meeting of any kind. President and Chairman are elected by the body over which they preside and may be removed by that body. A Master is elected by his lodge, but cannot be removed by it, only by the Grand Master or Grand lodge. The presiding officer is bound by the rules of order adopted by the body and by its by-laws. A lodge cannot pass by-laws to alter, amend or curtail the powers of a Master. Its by-laws are subject to approval by the proper Grand Lodge committee or by the Grand Master; seldom are any approved which infringe upon his ancient prerogatives and power; in those few instances in which improper by-laws have been approved, subsequent rulings have often declared the Master right in disregarding them.

Grand Lodges differ in their interpretation of some of the "ancient usages and customs" of the fraternity; what applies in one Jurisdiction does not necessarily apply in another. But certain powers of a Master are so well recognized that they may be considered universal. The occasional exceptions, if any, prove the rule.

The Master may congregate his lodge when he pleases, and for that purpose he wishes, provided, it does not interfere with the laws of the Grand Lodge. For instance, he may assemble his lodge at a Special Communication to confer degrees, at his pleasure; but he must not, in so doing, contravene that requirement of the Grand Lodge which calls for proper notice to the brethren, nor may a Master confer a degree in less than the statutory time following a preceding degree without a dispensation from the Grand Master.

The Master has the right of presiding over and controlling his lodge, and only the Grand Master or his Deputy may suspend him. He may put any brother in the East to preside or to confer a degree; he may then resume the gavel at his pleasure—even in the middle of a sentence if he wants to! But even when he has delegated authority temporarily the Master is not relieved from responsibility for what occurs in his lodge.

It is the Master's right to control lodge business and work. It is in a very real sense his lodge. He decides all points of order and no appeal from his decision may be taken to the lodge. He can initiate and terminate debate at his pleasure, he can second any motion, propose any motion, vote twice in case of a tie (not universal), open and close at his pleasure, with the usual exception that he may not open a Special Communication at an hour earlier than that given in the notice, or a Stated Communication earlier than the hour stated in the by-laws, without dispensation from the Grand Master. He is responsible only to the Grand Master and the Grand lodge, and obligations he assumed when he was installed, his conscience and his God.

The Master has the undoubted right to say who shall enter, and who must leave, the lodge room. He may deny any visitor entrance; indeed, he may deny a member the right to enter his own lodge, but he must have a good and sufficient reason therefor, otherwise his Grand Lodge will unquestionably rule such a drastic step arbitrary and punish accordingly. Per contra, if he permits the entry of a visitor to whom some member has objected, he may also subject himself to Grand Lodge discipline. In other words, his power to admit and exclude is absolute; his right to admit or exclude is protected by the pledges he takes at his installation and the rules of his Grand Lodge.

A very important power of a Master is that of appointing committees. No lodge may appoint a committee. The lodge may pass a resolution that a committee be appointed, but the selection of that committee is an inherent right of the Master. He is, ex officio, a member of all committees he appoints. The reason is obvious; he is responsible for the conduct of his lodge to the Grand Master and the Grand Lodge. If the lodge could appoint committees and act upon their recommendations, the Master would be in the anomalous position of having great responsibilities, and no power to carry out their performance.

The Master, and only the Master, may order a committee to examine a visiting brother. It is his responsibility to see that no cowan or eavesdropper comes within the tiled door. Therefore, it is for him to pick a committee in which he has confidence. So, also, with the committees which report upon petitioners. He is responsible for the accuracy, the fair-mindedness, the speed, and the intelligence of such investigations. It is, therefore, for him to say to whom shall be delegated this necessary and important work.

It is generally, not exclusively, held that only the Master can issue a summons. The dispute, where it exists, is over the right of members present at a stated communication to summons the whole membership.

It may now be interesting to look for a moment at some matters in which the Worshipful Master is not supreme and catalog a few things he may not do.

The Master, and only the Master, appoints the appointive officers in his lodge. In most Jurisdictions, he may remove such appointed officers at his pleasure. But he cannot suspend, or deprive of his station or place, any officer elected by the lodge. The Grand Master or his Deputy may do this; the Worshipful Master may not.

A Master may not spend lodge money without the consent of the lodge. As a matter of convenience, a Master frequently does pay out money in sudden emergencies, looking to the lodge to reimburse him. But he cannot spend any lodge funds without the permission of the lodge.

A Master cannot accept a petition or confer a degree without the consent of the lodge. It is for the lodge, not the Master, to say from what men it will receive an application, upon what candidates' degrees shall be conferred. The Master has the same power to reject with the black ball that is possessed by any member, but no power whatever to accept any candidate against the will of the lodge.

The lodge, not the Master, must approve or disapprove the minutes of the preceding meeting. The Master cannot approve them; had he that power he might, with the connivance of the Secretary, "run wild" in his lodge and still his minutes would show no trace of his improper conduct. But the Master may refuse to put a motion to confirm or approve minutes which he believes to be inaccurate or incomplete; in this way he can prevent a careless, headstrong Secretary from doing what he wants with his minutes! Should a Master refuse to permit minutes to be confirmed, the matter would naturally be brought before the Grand Lodge or the Grand Master for settlement.

A Master cannot suspend the by-laws. He must not permit the lodge to suspend the by-laws. If the lodge wishes to change them, the means are available, not in suspension but in amendment.

An odd exception may be noted, which has occurred in at least one Grand Jurisdiction and doubtless may occur in others. A very old lodge adopted by-laws shortly after it was constituted, which by-laws were approved by a young Grand Lodge before that body had, apparently, devoted much attention to these important rules.

For many years this lodge carried in its by-laws an "order of business" which specified, among other things, that following the reading of the minutes, the next business was balloting. At the same meeting of this lodge was early (seven o'clock) this by-law worked a hardship for years, compelling brethren who wished to vote to hurry to lodge, often at great inconvenience.

At last, a Master was elected who saw that the by-laws interfered with his right to conduct the business of the lodge as he thought proper. He balloted at what he thought the proper time; the last order of business, not the first. An indignant committee of Past Masters, who preferred the old order, applied to the Grand Master for relief. The Grand Master promptly ruled that "order of business" in the by-laws could be no more than suggestive, not mandatory; and that the Worshipful Master had power to order a ballot on a petition at the hour which seemed to him wise, provided—and this was stressed—that he ruled wisely, and did not postpone a ballot until after a degree, or until so late in the evening that brethren wishing to vote upon it had left the lodge room.

A Worshipful Master has no more right to invade the privacy which shrouds the use of the black ball, or which conceals the reason for an objection to an elected candidate receiving the degrees, than the humblest member of the lodge. He cannot demand disclosure of action or motive from any brother, and should he do so, he would be subject to the severest discipline from Grand Lodge. Grand Lodges usually argue that a dereliction of duty by a brother who possesses the ability and character to attain the East, is worse than that of some less well-informed brother. The Worshipful Master receives great honor, has great privileges, enjoys great prerogatives and powers. Therefore, he must measure up to great responsibilities.

A Worshipful Master cannot resign. Vacancies occur in the East through death, suspension by a Grand Master, expulsion from the fraternity. No power can make a Master attend to his duties if he desires to neglect them. If he will not, or does not, attend to them, the Senior Warden presides. He is, however, still Senior Warden; he does not become Master until elected and installed.

In broad outline, these are the important and principal powers and responsibilities of a Worshipful Master, considered entirely from the standpoint of the "ancient usages and customs of the Craft." Nothing is here said of the moral and spiritual duties which devolve upon a Master.

Volumes might be and some have been written upon how a Worshipful Master should preside, in what ways he can "give the brethren good and wholesome instruction," and upon his undoubted moral responsibility to do his best to leave his lodge better then he found it. Here we are concerned only with the legal aspect of his powers and duties.

Briefly, then, if he keeps within the laws, resolutions, and edicts of his Grand lodge on the one hand, and the Landmarks, Old Charges, Constitutions and "ancient usages and customs" on the other, the power of the Worshipful Master is that of an absolute monarch. His responsibilities and his duties are those of an apostle of Light!

He is a gifted brother who can fully measure up to the use of his power and the power of his leadership.

APPENDIX B

WHY FREEMASONRY HAS ENEMIES
THE SHORT TALK BULLETIN
The Masonic Service Association of the United States
Volume 27 Number 5
May 1949
Author Unknown

Say "Anti-Masonry" to the average American Mason and he will think you speak only of the Morgan affair of 1826. So many books have been written on this, so many speeches made about it, so many study clubs have discussed it, that it is pretty much in the class with political oratory — interesting once, but a bore when much repeated!

Anti-Masonry neither began nor ended with the Morgan affair. The fraternity has always had its enemies and, unless the world reforms spiritually, doubtless always will. BUT WHY?

Doubtless there are many answers. Many roads may wind around a mountain — they must meet at the top. No matter how many separate causes for the hatred, dislike, enmity which men have conceived — and some still do — for the Gentle Craft, all these mistaken ideas may be referred to one cause.

Examine just a few of the exhibitions of anti-Masonry, other than the Morgan affair — which was a sporadic explosion, not a deep - rooted and poisonous plant.

Mussolini, Hitler, Franco, Stalin could not permit the existence of a society which is predicated upon the brotherhood of man; they were, and are, too much committed to a society predicated upon a police power which knows no mercy and has but one object; the destruction of people, ideas, and organizations which do not believe that man is nothing, the State (and its ruler or rulers) everything.

Mussolini's anti-Masonic feeling was expressed in his doctrine of conflict, which does not even mention the Craft:

"Humanity is still and always an abstraction of time and space; men are still not brothers, do not want to be and evidently cannot be. Peace is hence absurd, or rather it is a pause in war. There is something that binds man to his destiny of struggling, against either his fellows or himself. The motives for the struggle may change indefinitely, they may be economic, religious, political, sentimental, But the legend of Cain and Abel seems to be the inescapable reality, while brotherhood is a fable man listen to during the bivouac and the truce."

General Erich Ludendorff wrote a booklet against Freemasonry of which more than a hundred thousand copies were sold. Too long to quote here, the reader may get an idea of its contents from some of his words.

"Masonry brings its members into conscious subjection to the Jews...... it trains them to become venal Jews.... German Masonry is a branch of organized international Masonry the headquarters of which are in New York.... there also is the seat of Jewish world power...."

Ludendorff blamed Freemasons for bringing America into World War I, helped by the Jesuits, B'nai B'rith and the Grand

Lodge of New York! This, he stated, was done to destroy Austria Hungary, a Catholic world power. Had it not been for Freemasonry, Germany would have won the war — Kaiser Wilhelm and Czar Nicholas lost their thrones because they were not Freemasons — and so on and on and on for eighty-two pages of "Annihilation of Freemasonry Through revelation of its Secrets!"

Not all anti-Masonry has had causes so fundamental, which lie so deep; small jealousies and little rascals have started anti - Masonic movements; several religions have fought and, indeed, now fight the Craft, as sinful and ungodlike. The opposition of the Catholic church, based on the Papal Bull of 1738, many times renewed, expanded, explained, and emphasized, is well known. The Lutheran church as a whole has been unfriendly to the Craft and certain Synods rabid against it. The Mormon church has been anti-Masonic ever since hundreds of Mormons were expelled from Masonry by the Grand Lodge of Illinois. Even the Gentle Quakers have opposed Freemasonry and not always gently!

When organized religion has disputed with Freemasonry, it is largely because of the thought that Masonic teaching of "that natural religion in which all men agree" might take the place of that which it espoused; knowing that the fraternity operated by means of a secret ritual, obligations, religious beliefs and the doctrine that all men of whatever faith might worship a Great Architect of the Universe around a common Altar, Freemasonry became a rival! Just as science disputes with no religion, so Freemasonry does not now and never has questioned any man's faith. There has never been an anti-clerical party composed only of Masons; there have been anti-Masonic parties in many clerical circles. As late as 1896 an anti-Masonic party convened at Trent. In the *Builder*, April, 1918, George W. Baird, P.G.M. District of Columbia, reports that the general and particular aims of this council were to wage war on Masonry as an institution; on Masons as individuals, in all countries and places where the order exists; to wage war on Masonry as a body, by collecting supposed documents and facts; assertions of perjured Masons as evidence and thus bring to light or rather to coin, by means of the press or special publications, all the misdeeds of the fatal institution; all the demoralizing influences it exercises; through obscene or sacrilegious rites, corruption and occult conspiracies of man and civilization; to wage war on individual Masons by opposing them in every phase of their existence, in their homes, in their industries, in their commerce, in their professional vocations, in all their endeavors to participate in public life, local or general, etc.

The first anti-Masonic campaign — if it can be called that — in the American Colonies occurred in 1737. According to an account published in the Pennsylvania Gazette (Benjamin Franklin's paper) an apothecary duped a young man (Daniel Reese) who had expressed a desire to be a Freemason, into a false and ridiculous ceremony, ending in a scene in which the devil was supposed to appear. When the young man refused to be frightened, the "devil" became angry and threw a pan of flaming spirits on the candidate, who died of burns three days later.

Freemasons, though innocent, were blamed and the incident (if death can be called and incident!) spread far and wide to the serious but not too lengthy embarrassment of Masons of the City of Brotherly Love.

There were a few sporadic attacks in the Colonial press against Freemasonry, including one in Boston in 1751, but no real opposition of any moment in this nation until the Morgan affair of 1826. (See *Short Talk Bulletin* of March 1933 and February 1946.)

But the Colonies were not to escape prejudice, even if unorganized, for Pritchard's *Masonry Dissected* (1730) and *Jachin and Boaz* (1762) both had wide circulation, the latter pamphlet being reprinted here more than a dozen times; one edition was printed in Spanish in Philadelphia as late as 1822.

These "expose's" purporting to print the ritual, ceremonies, and "secrets" of Freemasonry (invaluable now as giving clues to practices and words otherwise lost in the mist of the years) were then intended as body blows to the Ancient Craft. In early days, all Freemasonry was kept secret — places of meetings; men who belonged; candidates proposes, were all considered to be "esoteric." Hence there was a great curiosity on the part of the public and a large circulation of pamphlets designed to injure the fraternity by "exposing" its charter, ritual, and secrets. Today, few would look at and less would buy such a pamphlet on a newsstand — then, the public demanded these in quantities.

Like all such, the motive of their publication—whether revenge for fancied slights or avarice — kept them from being too seriously considered by the better educated and thinking class.

In England, Pritchard's *Masonry Dissected* raised a storm when it was published and was reflected even in the songs of the day. An actress in 1765 offered the following, as coming from the anti - Masonic Scald Miserable Masons:

"Next for the secret of their own wise making,
Hiram and Boaz and Grand Master Jachin;
Poker and tongs-the sign-the word-the stroke

'Tis all a nothing and 'tis all a joke!
Nonsense on nonsense! Let them storm and rail
Here's the whole history of the mop and pail
For 'tis the sense of more than half the town
Their secret is-a bottle at the Crown!"

Although inspired by the Morgan affair, the letters of John Quincy Adams had an anti-Masonic effect long after Morgan was forgotten. President Adams was never a Freemason; we have his own words as proof of that. That he was an implacable enemy of the institution is shown by his *Letters on the Masonic Institution* published in book form in Boston in 1847. His enmity of the fraternity sprang from his belief in the reality of the "murder" of Morgan, the activities of the anti-Masonic party and his own great credulity and strong prejudice. His character as a man, his service to his county, his exhaustless energy made serious his attacks on Freemasonry, even though he displayed a woeful ignorance of the Order, its principles, practices, history, and accomplishments.

John Quincy Adams is long gathered to his fathers. His "letters" remain largely unread in libraries and in the minds of historians. He did the fraternity harm once, but, judged by the perspective of a century, it was without permanent effect.

These are but the slightest thumb-nail sketches of a few of the outbreaks against Freemasonry. In all countries since the organization of the Mother Grand lodge, there have been these ebullitions of passions and prejudice; in some lands, tortures and burnings; destructions of Masonic property, imprisonment of Masons, especially in World War II.

These persecutions have had a hundred underlying causes; avarice, jealousy, desire for notoriety, disappointment, envy, the belief that he climbs high who climbs ruthlessly, the need for a scrape-goat: the list is endless. But all, in the last analysis, boil down to one cause, as the greater swallows the less, the large encompasses the little, the race includes all its blood strains, so the reason for the enmity of Freemasons and Freemasonry, encompassing all of many causes, is simple.

There is always a conflict between any two opposing beliefs, doctrines, dogmas, religions, philosophies, political systems. For hundreds of years organized religion fought science; the doctrine of the divine right of kings ran headlong into the doctrine of the equality of man; today we see Democracy and Communism in a cold war to the death; less spectacular but none the less real has been the split of Lincoln's famous words, resulting in the opposition of those who believe in government by the people, to those who believe only in government of the people, by the governor!

Freemasonry is a philosophy which cannot exist side by side with certain ideologies. Either the latter must sink, or Freemasonry must be banished. Wherever men have believed that one man or some men are above the law which applies to the many; wherever as government is by men and not by law, Freemasonry is anathema, must be persecuted, thrown out, dispersed, done away.

Freemasonry stands and has always stood for freedom of political thought; for freedom of religious thought; for the dignity, importance and worth of the individual. In Freemasonry there is neither high nor low— "We meet upon the level." In Freemasonry there is no compulsion; a man must come to it and be of it "of his own free will and accord." In Freemasonry is no religious sect: men of all religions or of no religion, join hands in kneeling about a common Altar erected to the Great Architect of the Universe, by which name each can worship the God he knows.

Such a plan, such a doctrine, such a brotherhood, cannot but be inimical to the selfish, the crooked, the power-hungry, the dictator, the religion which opposes any doctrine but its own, the self-seeking, the envious, the coward, the prejudiced, the passionate and the dishonest.

The reason for all the attacks on Masonry, no matter how attempted or by whom accomplished, can be expressed in a word...

The word is FEAR. Fear of what?
OF FREEDOM OF THOUGHT!

APPENDIX C

SUGAR-COATING MASONIC EDUCATION
THE SHORT TALK BULLETIN
The Masonic Service Association of the United States
Volume 7 Number 9
September 1929
Author Unknown

However improper curiosity may be as a principal motive for applying for the degrees, it is probable that no man ever passed through the West Gate for his initiation as an Entered Apprentice without an eager desire to know "what will happen next?"

Immediately thereafter the candidate usually develops a healthy curiosity as to the "why" of that which "happened next." Entered Apprentices and Fellowcrafts are generally hungry for explanations of the reasons and for the motives behind the words and acts of a degree.

Man is incurably curious; his desire to know and to understand is the mainspring of invention, discovery, civilization and progress; it is the driving force which leads men to learn.

Worshipful Masters can — and many of them do — make use of the desire to know, to make better Masons of the brethren of their lodges. Masters are charged with the duty of giving the Craft "good and wholesome instruction," or causing the same to be done. But one of the principal methods developed by Masonic educators, the "educational meeting," is a method of instruction more injured than helped by its name! For many brethren had boyish experiences with "education" which led them to associate with that word a process which is dry, dull and uninteresting.

What is here called a "sugar coated" Masonic educational meeting is just the reverse; interesting, intriguing, alive, vital, and satisfying a great curiosity. lodges which have tried any of the educational experiments here listed usually repeat them, and almost invariably the repetition is to a "packed house."

Here are some suggestions for "sugar coated" educational meetings; all of them have been tried, and all found successful methods of interesting the Craft in the various phases of Freemasonry.

1. BREAKING RULES TO MEND THEM

Certain unwritten rules of Masonic conduct, as well as some specified by Grand lodges, become so much a matter of custom in lodges that many brethren lose sight of the reasons therefore, if, indeed, they ever knew them.

The Worshipful Master may arrange a program in which a number of brethren, instructed beforehand, to deliberately commit or attempt to commit infractions of the rules. When the error is made, the Master, or some previously instructed brother (a Past Master), explains the mistake and the reason for the rule. For instance, in most Jurisdictions it is not considered courteous for a brother to pass between the Worshipful Master and the Alter (except when in the process of conferring a degree). When the instructed brother crosses the lodge between the Altar and the East, the Master may admonish the "culprit" that it is not considered proper, and call upon some previously instructed Past Master to explain that, in theory, the Great Light and the Square and Compasses on the Altar; are dedicated to God, the Master and the Craft; and, therefore at no time should his view of them be interrupted. A brother who attempts to leave the room during a ballot may be corrected and the reason given; Grand Lodges usually hold that a ballot on a petition, interrupted by anyone entering or leaving the room, is invalid, since such an action may interfere with the secrecy of said ballot. Similarly, a brother balloting may object to the officer in charge of the ballot box standing so close to the altar that he might discover how a brother votes. Either or both of these incidents provide an excellent opportunity for a little talk upon the sacredness and secrecy of the Masonic ballot, and its importance. Others are speaking more than twice to the same question, speaking without being recognized, speaking without rising, addressing an individual brother or the lodge instead of the Master, making a motion to appoint a committee with certain specified personnel, offering a resolution "to adjourn" or to "lay a motion on the table," are suggested infractions of Masonic law and custom, all of which may be corrected in an educational meeting in an interesting way.

2. DISSECTING A DEGREE

Especially recommended for lodges which have little work to do is the dissection and explanation of the first section of any degree. A pretend candidate is initiated, and the ceremony interrupted at each stage by some brother who offers a little explanation of the symbolism of that part of the degree; entry, circumambulation, rite of destitution, the antiquity of the Apron, origin of the Lesser Lights, etc. Such dissection and exposition of parts of a degree require some little study by those who take part, but by giving each brother who offers an interruption only one subject, the work of preparation is minimized, and the variety increased by having many take part.

It is suggested here that inquiry be first made of the District Deputy, or the Grand Master; in some Jurisdictions the practice of using a pretend candidate has been frowned upon, as derogatory to the dignity of our ceremonies. When it is explained that the purpose of the idea is educational, however, it is probable that no difficulty will be experienced in obtaining cooperation from those in authority.

3. YOU MUST - YOU MUST NOT!

The average lodge member knows little about Masonic Law. The very term "Jurisprudence" seems repellent. Yet Masonic Law is intensely interesting and may be made to appear so to the lodge by any brother who will devote a little time and attention to developing a talk on those parts of our legal system which most intimately touch the brethren. Masonic Law is vastly different from civil law; most Masonic Law is a matter of "thou shalt" rather than "thou shalt not." A few salient points chosen for their interest to the average Mason, and explained; first, as to their origin; and second, as to their use or necessity will interest the lodge. It is not at all an arduous task for a clever brother to arrange such a talk. He may use any good book on Jurisprudence as a foundation, Mackey or Pound for choices, as both are complete and concise.

4. COMPETITION IS THE LIFE OF — EDUCATION!

The more brethren that take part in an educational meeting, the greater the enjoyment. No scheme for an educational meeting yet developed exceeds the lodge contest in this respect, since it gives everyone in the lodge room an opportunity to participate. The educational contest is conducted by a Master of Ceremonies asking a series of questions, carefully prepared in advance, the correct answers to which can be given in a word or two, a date or a name. Supplied with paper and pencils, the brethren write and number their answers to the questions, as they are asked. Then they exchange papers, the correct answers are read, and the brethren mark the replies "right" or "wrong" according to the facts. The winners, of course, are those who have the greatest number, the next greatest and the third greatest answered correctly. Interest in such a contest is increased by offering prizes. These may be very inexpensive; a good Masonic book, a subscription to a Masonic Magazine, a Masonic lapel pin are all appreciated.

The questions should not be complex; answers should be facts, not opinions. For instance, "In what lodge was George Washington raised?" "Who is the Grand Master in this state?" "How old is this lodge?" "How many lodges in our Grand lodge Jurisdiction?" These are the type of questions that need only a word or two for an answer with facts. Such questions as "Why do some think Masonry is a religion?" should not be included, since any answer must be an opinion, not a fact. Questions like "Explain the part Freemasonry played in the Revolution" should not be asked, as it would require a lengthy reply. In giving out the correct answers, a clever Master of Ceremonies will be able to offer some "good and wholesome instruction" of Masonic value; for instance, if the question is: "How many landmarks are recognized in this Jurisdiction?" If the correct answer is "twenty-five," the Master of Ceremonies may explain that some Jurisdictions have less, others more; that many Jurisdictions have adopted Mackey's list, while others have condensed Mackey's twenty-five into a lesser number; which, never the less contains all of Mackey's points, and so on.

A lodge debate will draw a crowd and keep it interested for the best part of an hour, with pleasure and profit to all. Debating teams may be composed of two or more brethren on each side of the issue; two to a side usually produces a snappier debate than three. Some questions of universal Masonic interest should be chosen, such as "Resolved, that dual membership is advantageous to the fraternity," or "Resolved, that Masonic trials are better conducted by a Grand lodge Commission than a particular lodge."

Such debates should be planned well in advance. An impromptu debate often produces amusing results. Two captains are chosen; each captain chooses six debaters. The Master then announces the subject. Each debater is given two minutes and must sit down when the gong rings at the end of his time, even if in the middle of a sentence. The simpler the subject, the livelier the debate. Such questions as "Resolved, that this lodge should start a library," or "Resolved, that the fees for the degrees are too low" (or too high!) will produce more debate than more abstruse questions, because brethren seldom argue well on difficult matters unless they have previously spent some time in preparation.

It is not suggested that these "sugar coated" methods of holding Masonic educational meetings should replace older, tried and true forms in which some learned brother delivers an address upon a Masonic subject or presents an illustrated lecture. The speaker and the lecturer we have always had with us; illustrated lectures on Masonic subjects will always be of interest to the Craft, as will the well-conceived and delivered address.

But we tire of anything in too great qualities. Quail is considered the best eating, yet it is a restauranteur's tradition that no man can eat a quail a day for a month!

144

The Masonic educational meeting conducted on new, different lines — of which the above list is only suggestive, not complete — will largely "take the curse off" the word "educational" meeting. Brethren who are provided with "sugar coated" education do not stay away on "educational nights" but come out in full force. Once the lodge members begin thinking "I wonder what new idea the Master will spring tonight!" When an educational meeting is announced, the Stewards will have to go to the basement after extra chairs.

Sugar coated pills do the same work as those more difficult to swalow — and they are much easier to take!

APPENDIX D

LODGE COURTESIES
THE SHORT TALK BULLETIN
The Masonic Service Association of the United States
Volume 2 Number 8
August 1924
Author Unknown

Conventions are the rules which society makes for itself, without the force of law, by which its members live together with the least friction. It is not a sin to eat with one's knife or to keep one's hat on in the house. But these are not "good form" or good manners.

Masonry has developed its own conventions, by which its members act in lodge and the anteroom. Not to proceed according to their dictates is not a Masonic offense, it is merely a lack of Masonic manners.

As you passed through the Third Degree you received instructions in the Ritual and the obligation. You were carefully taught those essential things which a man must know in order to be a Mason. But unless you belong to a most unusual lodge, or had a most wise brother for a mentor, it is doubtful if you were told much about these little niceties of lodge conduct. You are supposed to attend your lodge and learn by observation.

Not all brethren are observing, however. It is common to see some brother, old enough in Masonry to know better, crossing the lodge room between the Altar and the East. He might have observed that his brethren did not do it; but it is more difficult to note the absence of an act than to take cognizance of something done.

Brethren do not pass between the Altar and the East in lodge. It is a convention; there is no penalty for its infraction. It is a courtesy offered the Master. It is rooted in the theory that, as the Great Lights and the Charter of the lodge are essential to the regularity of the meeting, as these are the particular care of the Master, and as their place is upon the Altar, the Master should never be interrupted in his plain view of them, even for an instant.

Well informed brethren do not take seats in the East without invitation. All brethren within the tiled door are equal; the officers are the servants of their brethren and not their superiors. All seats, then, might well be considered open to all. But Masonry exacts long services of her officers; Past Masters have worked hard and long for the lodge they love. The Master recognizes their devotion and their loyalty with a special word of welcome, and an invitation to them to occupy a seat with him, in the East where they once sat. From this pretty custom has developed the invitation to a "seat in the East" to any distinguished visitor, or some member the Master wishes particularly to honor. If all in the lodge helped themselves to seats in the East, there would be no opportunity for the Master to offer that courtesy.

Brethren who respect the formalities of their lodge will not enter it undressed; that is, without their apron, or while putting that apron on. The spectacle of a brother walking up to the Altar, tying the strings and adjusting his apron while the Master waits for his salute, is not a pretty one. A man who entered church putting on his collar and tying his necktie would hardly be arrested, but he would surely receive unflattering comment. The strangeness of the new badge of a

Mason and unfamiliarity with its meaning cause many to forget that it is as important to a Mason in lodge as clean linen, properly adjusted, is to the man in the street.

The Worshipful Master in the East occupies the most exalted position in the lodge. A lodge which does not honor its Master, not because of what he himself may be, but on account of the honor given him, is lacking in Masonic courtesy. The position he occupies, not the man, must be given the utmost respect, if the traditions of the fraternity are to be observed.

It is, therefore, to the Master, not to John Smith who happens to be the Master, that you offer a salute when you enter or retire from lodge. Like any other salute, this may be done courteously and as if you meant it, or perfunctorily as if you did not care. The man who puts one finger to his hat brim when he speaks to a woman on the street compares poorly with his well brought up neighbor who lifts his hat. Taking the hat off is the modern remains of the ancient custom of knights who removed their helmets in the presence of those they felt their friends, and thus, before those they wished to honor by showing that they trusted them. A man removes his hat before a woman to show his respect. Touching the brim is but a perfunctory salute. Similarly, the salute to the Master is your renewed pledge of fealty and service, your public recognition before all men, of your obligation. It is performed before the Master and the Altar to show him your veneration for his authority, your respect for all that for which he stands. To offer your salute as if you were in a hurry, too lazy properly to make it, or bored with its offering, is to be, Masonically, a bore.

A man in lodge is the servant of his brethren, if he engages in any lodge activity. Servants stand in the presence of their superiors. Therefore, no Mason sits while speaking, whether he addresses an officer or another brother. This does not refer to conversation on the benches during refreshment, but to discussion on the floor during business meeting.

During the refreshment the Master relinquishes the gavel to the Junior Warden in the South, which thus becomes, for the time being, constructively the East. All that has been said about the respect due the Master in the East applies now to the Junior Warden in the South.

It is illegal to enter or leave the room during a ballot; it is discourteous to leave during a speech, or during a degree, except at the several natural periods which end one section and begin another.

Smoking is permitted in some lodge rooms during the business meeting. Alas, there are some which do not interdict it during a degree! You will, of course, be governed here by the custom of your own lodge, although it is to be hoped you will never lend the weight of your opinion toward establishing the custom of smoking during the solemn ceremonies of a degree, unless, indeed, you would like to smoke in church!

A courteous brother does not refuse a request made in the name of the lodge. There are three duties which devolve upon the membership which are too often "the other fellow's business." Every lodge at some time has a knock upon the door from some visiting brother. This requires the services of two brethren from the lodge on the examination committee. Someone has to do that work. To decline it, on any ground whatever, is discourteous to the Master, to whom you have said, in effect, "I don't want to do my share; let George do it. I just want to sit here and enjoy myself while the other fellows do the work."

A degree cannot well be put on without the services of conductors. When you are assigned such a piece of work, it is a Masonic discourtesy to refuse, for the same reasons given above. And if you are selected as a member of the Fellowcraft 'team in the Master Mason degree, the only reason for not accepting is that of physical disability. Like other matters herein spoken of, refusal here is not a Masonic offense. Neither is it a legal offense to drink from a finger bowl, seat yourself at table before your hostess, or spit on your host's parlor floor! But the convention of good manners is what makes society pleasant, and Masonic good manners make lodge meetings pleasant.

One does not talk in church. God's House is not for social conversation; it is for worship and the learning of the lesson of the day. A good Mason does not talk during the conferring of a degree. The lodge room is then a Temple of the Great Architect of the Universe, with the brethren working therein doing their humble best to make better stones for His spiritual Temple. Good manners as well as reverence dictate silence and attention during the work; officers and degree workers cannot do their best if distracted by conversation, and the irreverence cannot help but be distressing to candidates.

There is a special lodge courtesy to be observed in all debates to any motion. One speaks to the Master; the Master is the lodge. One does not turn one's back on him to address the lodge without permission from him. One stands to order when addressing the chair; customs differ in various jurisdictions as to the method of salute, but some salute should always be given when addressing the Master. The spectacle of two brethren on their feet at the same time, arguing over a motion, facing each other and ignoring the Master, is not one which any Master should permit. But it is also one which no Master should have to prevent!

Failure to obey the gavel at once is a grave discourtesy. The Master is all powerful in the lodge. He can put or refuse to put any motion. He can rule any brother out of order on any subject at any time. He can say what he will, and what he will not, permit to be discussed. Brethren who think him unfair, arbitrary, unjust, or acting illegally, have redress; the Grand Lodge can be appealed to on any such matter. But in the lodge, the gavel, emblem of authority, is supreme. When a brother is rapped down, he should at once obey, without further discussion. It is very bad manners to do otherwise; indeed, it is close to the line between bad manners and a Masonic offense.

Failure to vote on a petition is so common in many jurisdictions that it may be considered stretching the list to include it under a heading of lodge discourtesies. In smaller lodges the Master probably requires the satisfaction of the law which provides that all brethren present vote. In larger ones, where there is much business, and many petitions, he may, and often does, declare the ballot closed after having asked, "Have all the brethren voted?" Even though he knows quite well that they have not all voted. This is not the place to discuss whether the Master is right or wrong in such action. But the brother who does not vote, because he is too lazy, or too indifferent, or for any other reason, is discourteous because he injures the ballot, its secrecy, its importance, and its value. Few brethren would be so thoughtless as to remain seated, or stand by their chairs, when a candidate is brought to light. Yet indifference to one's part in this solemn ceremony is less bad manners than indifference to the ballot; the former injures only a ceremony; the latter may injure the lodge, and by that injury, the fraternity.

It is a courtesy to the Master to advise him beforehand that you intend to offer thus and such a motion or wish to bring up thus and such a matter for discussion. You have the right to do it without apprising him in advance, just as he has the right to rule you out of order. But the Master may have plans of his own for that meeting, into which your proposed motion or discourse does not fit. Therefore, it is a courtesy to him, to ask him privately if you may be recognized for your purpose, and thus save him the disagreeable necessity of seeming arbitrary in a public refusal.

Lodge courtesies, like those of the profane world, are founded wholly in the Golden Rule. They oil the Masonic wheels and enable them to revolve without creaking. They smooth the path of all in the lodge and prove to all and sundry the truth of the ritualistic explanation of that "more noble and glorious purpose" to which we are taught to put the trowel.

APPENDIX E

"TRULY PREPARED"
THE SHORT TALK BULLETIN
The Masonic Service Association of the United States
Volume 4 Number 5
May 1926
Author Unknown

Why do so many Masons lose interest in Masonry and drift away from the lodge? Why do the majority retain only a nominal relation to the Craft? Why is it that hardly 10 per cent ever attend any meeting of the lodge, and a still smaller number take an active part in its affairs? What is the meaning of these facts, and how can the problem which they raise be solved?

Such questions are much in the minds of the leaders of the Craft everywhere. It is a condition, and not a theory, which confronts us. The influx of members during the Great War, and in the years following it, has subsided. In some states the number of initiates has fallen below pre-war days. The vast mass of those who came in on the impulse of war-time are now numbered among the casual Masons. The feeling grows that something is wrong, and that we must seek to set it right, if we are to have an alert and active Masonry.

Just now The Masonic Service Association is working on this problem with the leaders of the Grand Lodge of Massachusetts, and we beg to give here the findings arrived at, both as to the meaning of the fact and the method of dealing with it. Clearly, we have failed "to set the Craft to work and give them proper instruction." Else they would not drop out of our membership, or regard Masonry as merely another Order to "belong to" and nothing more. To that end, we must begin at the beginning and lay the basis of a real Masonic life.

What is needed is extra-ritualistic preparation of the man applying for the Degrees before, during, and after his reception into the lodge. Of the three the first, if not the most vital, is surely profoundly important, and it has been almost entirely neglected. Let any man recall, if he can, his state of mind regarding the Craft when he knocked at its door, and he will realize than he had but the faintest idea of what Masonry is and of what it meant to be initiated into it. The method now proposed takes account of that fact, and takes him in hand as soon as he has expressed a desire to join the lodge, and before he has made his application for the degrees.

In this way, by making strict inquiry of an aspirant for the degrees to see if he has in him the stuff of which a Mason may be made, no end of embarrassment may be avoided, and the Craft strengthened or protected accordingly. The first duty of the Committee, as well as the last, is to see whether or not the man before them has the qualities of character which will enable him to add to the good name and integrity of the Craft, and also whether he will actually make such a contribution. In short, is he in his daily life and acts going to be a Mason in fact or in name only?

Such information or impression can be obtained by examining him as to his attitude toward Masonry. Why is he applying? What induced him to take the step? What is his opinion of Masonry and upon what does his opinion rest? It should be emphasized, in plain terms, that his privilege of membership in the Craft carries with it certain obligations that will rest upon him toward the Craft. It must be explained to the applicant that it is the business on Masonry to teach the virtues of the moral life — chastity, charity, service — and his known attitude in regard to these matters ought to determine whether he is a man fit for the fellowship of the fraternity.

Also, care must be taken to impress upon the applicant the fact that the moral life obtains its sanction and authority from Spiritual Faith. He ought to be asked, not obtrusively but candidly and earnestly, his ideas regarding God. If he has not clearly confronted his mind with the Supreme Reality, he ought to be asked to do so. No man who is uncertain about God, or who treats the idea of God as a piece of lodge furniture, has any place in a Masonic lodge.

It is important that an applicant should know what duties devolve upon him as a member of a lodge. Such as acquaintance with the ritual and other items of Masonic information. Attendance upon the lodge as a duty, and whether or not he is in a position to attend. Whether he is willing to assist in the work of the lodge, by serving on Committees or otherwise. As to his financial obligation — can he afford what will be necessary for him to spend?

When his petition has been voted upon, along with his notice of election, the applicant ought to receive a copy of the pamphlet entitled *Preparation*, with the request that he read it carefully. After he has received the Entered Apprentice Degree he should be given a bird's-eye view of Masonry, so to put it, showing its geographical distribution in Grand lodges, both at home and abroad. He will realize that Masonry encircles the earth. He ought to be told of the leading men in the State and the Nation who are and have been masons, if only to let him see what kind and quality of men the Craft attracts and develops.

It is not an accident that Masonry lures strong men and makes them stronger. Its teachings are the basic principles of civilized society, the very ground-work of Church and State and Home. Every man needs to realize that the truths of Masonry are not secret, but only the method and symbols by which they are taught. The parts of our ceremonies which are secret ought to be pointed out, and the candidate cautioned about disclosing what he has received.

Those who "post" the candidate on the "work" of the Degree ought to tell him something of what it means, after the manner of the "intenders" in the old lodges of Scotland. Such a book as *The Symbolism of The Three Degrees*, by Street, is useful for this purpose, not that it should be read to the candidate, but its facts told to him as he goes along. He should know the use of the Tools of the Craft, the meaning of its Great Lights — especially the Great Light; its teaching about Brotherly Love, Relief, and Faith; Its cardinal virtues of Temperance, Fortitude, Prudence, Justice.

As in the Scottish lodges, the obligation should be explained, particularly the figurative character of its penalty, and the fashion in which the oath was sealed and why. He ought to know the due guard and sign of the degree, and when and how they are to be used in the lodge. It is not enough to tell him these facts. He ought to be fully clothed, and asked to enter and retire from the lodge in proper manner. A candidate is in novel surroundings, and while he does not remember all that is told him, it is not easy to forget what he acts out.

In like manner the Second Degree is to be studied, showing in what ways it differs from the First, in the greater inclusiveness of its obligation, as well as in its emphasis upon the arts and sciences, with particular reference to Geometry and its meaning and use by the Craft. The initiate is asked to read The Masonic Service Association Bulletin entitled *3-5-7* before taking the Third Degree. It is a pity that neither the ritual nor the lecture tells us the meaning of the Great Degree, which has in it the sublime secret of Masonry and of life itself. All effort must be made to get the initiate to grasp the truth with which it deals — the truth of the Eternal Life.

Having received the Degrees of Masonry, an initiate needs to know something of the regulations of the Craft, its Constitution, its Landmarks, and the nature and authority of the Grand Lodge under whose obedience he lives. It is only fair to tell him the relation of the Blue Lodge to other Masonic bodies, both York and Scottish, in a way to emphasize the supremacy of Craft Masonry. It will be useful for him to know that the Shrine, the Grotto, and other such organizations, while made up of Masons, are not Masonic any more than a Club made up of Masons is Masonic. More important still is the etiquette of the Craft, in the lodge and outside, and the discretion necessary in making himself known as a Mason, or in responding to the advances of others.

Such simple things about Masonry and how to use it ought to be taught every Mason in the lodge; and such extra-ritualistic instruction the Grand Lodge of Massachusetts proposes to give men who enter its fellowship — using the literature and other helps prepared by The Masonic Service Association. It is hoped that other Grand Lodges will take up the plan, or some other equally good, in simple fairness to men who are made Masons - that they may be duly and truly prepared for the better appreciation and service of the Craft. Some of us, looking back, wish very much that we had been thus set to work and taught the meanings and uses of our tools.

The adoption of such a plan by an old and great Grand Lodge marks a long step in the right direction — a new epoch in Masonic education, of which we have heard so much and seen so little result. It is like a dream come true, the full meaning of which few can realize save those who have worked and planned for years to see it become a fact. Such things we can do together, each borrowing from the wisdom of the other. Those of us who had to wait long and hard for information about Masonry which should have been taught us by our mother lodge, look with envy upon the young men of the Old Bay State.

APPENDIX F

PREPARATION
by Carl H. Claudy - 1925

You are preparing to become a Freemason.

How are you preparing? You have the ambition to put upon your breast a tiny pin, representing the Square and Compasses; an ambition to be known as a Master Mason; an ambition to join the great fraternity of which, perhaps, your father was a member; an ambition to be one of that large brotherhood of which you may have heard so much and of which you know so little.

So, you asked a friend, whom you knew to be a Freemason, how to proceed. He gave you a petition to fill out and sign. You were asked to declare your belief in God, and probably your friend explained to you that "God" here means the Supreme Architect of the Universe, call Him by what name you will. He may be to you God or Jehovah or Adonai or Buddha or Allah . . . it makes no difference to Freemasons by what Name you call Him, so there is within you the humble acknowledgment that you are a creature of His, and that He reigns over the heavens and the earth.

It is all very simple; the other questions are of a practical and mundane character and give you no hint of what a degree may be, in what sort of a ceremony of initiation you will participate, what kind of a fraternity Freemasonry is.

And so, there was no hint given you in the paper you signed as to what sort of preparation you should make to become a Freemason. Freemasonry jealously guards her reputation, which is of humility and self-effacement as well as of secrecy and good works.

Freemasonry does not advertise herself. While her contacts with the world are numerous and commonplace, she works so silently, so quietly, that the world knows little of her labors. You seldom hear Freemasonry discussed in public, and references to Freemasonry in the literature of all countries are so cunningly concealed, that you, and all others not members of the Craft, have almost nothing to guide you as to what you should do to and for yourself before you take your Entered Apprentice Degree.

But if you seek, you shall find, in Freemasonry as well as elsewhere. if the friend to whom you went for your petition is a well-informed Freemason — and not all good Freemasons are as well informed, or as articulate about what they know, as you might like — he will tell you certain things. in case he cannot or will not speak, some of those things are set down here.

You asked a friend to take your petition into his lodge. His lodge is his Masonic home. Around it clusters all those happy memories, all those beautiful thoughts, all those heart-searching experiences, which go with the word "home." You asked him, therefore, to pay you the complement of taking you into one of the sacred places of his life; in the hope that it will be, and the implied promise that if admitted it shall be, to you one of the sacred places of your life.

You asked not a stranger, but a friend, for this. And his first reply was to direct you to express yourself as to your belief in God.

It does not take a very clever man to see that with such a beginning — the call of friendship, the sacredness of home, and the belief in God — Freemasonry is not a joke, not a foolish fun organization, not a club of "good fellows"; not an organization to join as one would a Board of Trade, for business purposes, it is obvious to anyone who thinks, that Freemasonry must be dignified, beautiful, impressive, that it must have a real meaning, a real part to play in a man's life.

Therefore, Brother-to-be, make your preparations to become a Freemason as you would prepare for any other great and ennobling experience of life.

When your petition was signed and delivered, the matter was out of your hands. The lodge assigned a committee to ascertain if you are worthy, from their standpoint, to be of the lodge. Your name was voted on, in due time. You were elected. Now you are notified to present yourself at the West Gate for initiation.

When you go, go clean in mind, in body and in heart.

Take from your mind and cast away forever all thought that there is a "lodge goat" awaiting you, or that your friends are going to "have fun with you." There are fun-loving organizations which cast aside solemnity and spend most of their evenings in laughter and play. But in a Master Mason's lodge, never! There is not a word spoken, an action performed, which can hurt your dignity or your feelings; there is no torture, physical or mental, to degrade you or Freemasonry. There is no "horse play" or other unhappiness awaiting you.

What is done with you has a meaning; the part you play is symbolic and only intended to make a "deep and lasting impression on your mind" of truths, the full understanding of which make you a better man. Put all fear from your mind; remember that is among friends you go, and that the first question they asked you was of your belief in a common Father; men do not start thus who begin to play a joke.

Go clean in body, as you would go clean to a christening or a baptism, nor resent this instruction here; there is intended no insinuation that you are not always clean, but go made clean expressly for this ceremony; though you have but just come from the bath for the evening, go once more and bathe with the thought that you are preparing now for a great step, that the water which laves your body is also, symbolically, cleansing your mind and your heart. Put on your freshest linen, and let its spotlessness be symbolic of that spotlessness your thoughts should have. For if you neglect these things, you will be sorry, afterwards; what Freemasonry does to you is done to you, not your brethren that will be, and Freemasonry will mean more to you as you approach her Altar humbly and purified.

Finally, Brother-to-be, go with a humble and contrite heart. If it is in your power to do so, put from your heart all evil. If you have an enemy, make an effort to forgive him before you enter the portals of the Temple. If you have done a sin, do your best to honestly regret it before you pass through the West Gate. If you have wronged anyone, make up your mind to right the wrong; you will be the happier man later in the evening if you do. And just before you leave your home, go alone in a quiet room, and all unashamed, get upon your knees before that God in whom you believe, and ask His blessing upon what you are about to do. Pray humbly for the wit to understand what you are about to hear. Ask that it may be given to you to be a good Freemason, to be a brother to others who will be brothers to you, a real workman in the quarry, erecting to Him a Temple not made with hands.

So, shall you become an Entered Apprentice with the greatest benefit to your brethren, and real joy to yourself.

Thank you for buying this Cornerstone book!

For over 30 years now, we've tried to provide the
Masonic community with quality books on
Masonic education, philosophy, and general interest.
Your support means everything to us and
keeps us afloat. Cornerstone is by no means a large
company. We are a small family-owned publishing house
that depends on your support.

Please visit our website and have a look at the
many books we offer as well as the different
categories of books.

If your lodge, Grand Lodge, research lodge, book
club, or other body would like to have quality
Cornerstone books to sell or distribute, write us. We
can give you outstanding books, prices, and service.

Thanks again!

Cornerstone Book Publishers
1cornerstonebooks@gmail.com
http://cornerstonepublishers.com

More Masonic Books from Cornerstone

The Particular Nature of Freemasons
by Michael R. Poll
6x9 Softcover 156 pages
ISBN 9781613423462

The Scottish Rite Papers
*A Study of the Troubled History of the Louisiana and
US Scottish Rite in the Early to Mid-1800s*
by Michael R. Poll
6x9 Softcover 240 pages
ISBN 9781613423448

Measured Expectations
The Challenges of Today's Freemasonry
by Michael R. Poll
6×9 Softcover 180 pages
ISBN: 978-1613422946

A Masonic Evolution
The New World of Freemasonry
by Michael R. Poll
6×9 Softcover 176 pages
ISBN: 978-1-61342-315-8

A Lodge at Labor
Freemasons and Masonry Today
by Michael R. Poll
6×9 Softcover 180 pages
ISBN: 978-1-61342-325-7

Cornerstone Book Publishers
www.cornerstonepublishers.com

More Masonic Books from Cornerstone

In His Own (w)Rite
by Michael R. Poll
6×9 Softcover 176 pages
ISBN: 1613421575

Seeking Light
The Esoteric Heart of Freemasonry
by Michael R. Poll
6×9 Softcover 156 pages
ISBN: 1613422571

An Encyclopedia of Freemasonry
by Albert Mackey
Revised by William J. Hughan and Edward L. Hawkins
Foreword by Michael R. Poll
8.5 x 11, Softcover 2 Volumes 960 pages
ISBN 1613422520

Living Freemasonry
A Better Path to Travel
by Michael R. Poll
6x9 Softcover 180 pages
ISBN 99781934935958

Robert's Rules of Order: Masonic Edition
Revised by Michael R. Poll
6 x 9 Softcover 212 pages
ISBN 1887560076

Cornerstone Book Publishers
www.cornerstonepublishers.com

www.ingramcontent.com/pod-product-compliance
Lightning Source LLC
Chambersburg PA
CBHW060228030426
42335CB00014B/1371